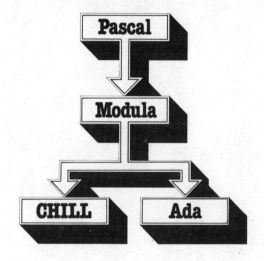

THE PROGRAMMING LANGUAGES

THE PROGRAMMING LANGUAGES

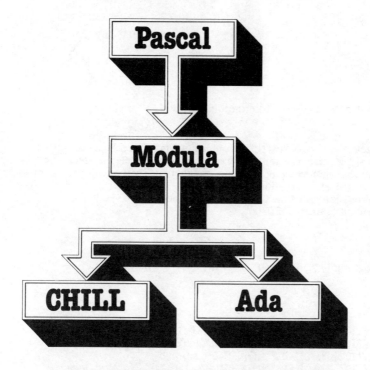

C.H. Smedema P. Medema M. Boasson

The Philips Group of Companies, The Netherlands

Prentice-Hall  International

Englewood Cliffs, New Jersey   London   New Delhi   Rio de Janeiro
Singapore   Sydney   Tokyo   Toronto   Wellington

ISBN 0-13-729756 4

PRENTICE-HALL INTERNATIONAL, INC., *London*
PRENTICE-HALL OF AUSTRALIA PTY. LTD., *Sydney*
PRENTICE-HALL CANADA, INC., *Toronto*
PRENTICE-HALL OF INDIA PRIVATE LIMITED, *New Delhi*
PRENTICE-HALL OF JAPAN, INC., *Tokyo*
PRENTICE-HALL OF SOUTHEAST ASIA PTE. LTD., *Singapore*
PRENTICE-HALL INC., *Englewood Cliffs, New Jersey*
PRENTICE-HALL DO BRASIL LTDA., *Rio de Janeiro*
WHITEHALL BOOKS LIMITED, *Wellington, N.Z.*

Printed in the United Kingdom
by A. Wheaton & Co. Ltd, Exeter

10 9 8 7 6 5 4 3 2 1

CONTENTS

Preface   4

1. Introduction

1.1 Trends in programming language design   7
1.2 Trends in applications   10
1.3 Trends in programming environments   10
1.4 Overview of Pascal, Modula, CHILL and Ada   11

2. Pascal

2.1 Introduction   14
2.2 Types   16

    2.2.1 Introduction   16
    2.2.2 Constant definitions   18
    2.2.3 Enumeration types   18
    2.2.4 Subrange types   20
    2.2.5 Structured types   20
    2.2.6 Array types   21
    2.2.7 Record types   21
    2.2.8 Set types   23
    2.2.9 File types   25
    2.2.10 Pointer types   26

2.3 Statements   28
2.4 Subprograms   29
2.5 Pascal extensions   34
2.6 Pascal descendants   37

3. Modula

3.1 Introduction   39
3.2 Types   41
3.3 Statements   42
3.4 Subprograms   44
3.5 Modules   45

3.6 Processes 49
3.7 Communication between processes 51
3.8 Device communication 57
3.9 Differences between Modula and Modula-2 62

4. CHILL

4.1 Introduction 66
4.2 Types 68

    4.2.1 Introduction 68
    4.2.2 Constant definitions 68
    4.2.3 Variable declarations 70
    4.2.4 Simple types 70
    4.2.5 Structured types 71
    4.2.6 Array types 71
    4.2.7 String types 72
    4.2.8 Record types 73
    4.2.9 Set types 76
    4.2.10 Pointer types 76
    4.2.11 Procedure types 78
    4.2.12 Representation specification 79
    4.2.13 New types and type compatibility 80

4.3 Statements 82
4.4 Subprograms 85
4.5 Modules 87
4.6 Processes 91
4.7 Communication between processes 93

    4.7.1 Introduction 93
    4.7.2 Regions 94
    4.7.3 Buffers 95
    4.7.4 Signals 97

4.8 Exceptions 99
4.9 Piecewise compilation 102

5. Ada

5.1 Introduction 104

5.2 Types   105

    5.2.1 Introduction   105
    5.2.2 Variable declarations   106
    5.2.3 Constant definitions   106
    5.2.4 Simple types   107
    5.2.5 Structured types   108
    5.2.6 Array types   108
    5.2.7 String types   109
    5.2.8 Record types   110
    5.2.9 Access types   113
    5.2.10 Private types   114
    5.2.11 Representation specification   114
    5.2.12 Derived types and type compatibility   116
    5.2.13 Overloading   117

5.3 Expressions and statements   117
5.4 Subprograms   121
5.5 Packages and private types   124

    5.5.1 Introduction   124
    5.5.2 Information hiding   124
    5.5.3 Private types   126

5.6 Tasks   129
5.7 Communication between tasks   131
5.8 Exceptions   136
5.9 Separate compilation   138
5.10 Generics   139

Bibliography   142

Index   144

PREFACE

Progress in programming languages has not stopped since the introduction, some 25 years ago, of languages like FORTRAN, ALGOL 60 and COBOL. A major step forward occurred around 1970 when Pascal was defined. Other modern programming languages like Modula (1976), CHILL (1980) and Ada† (1983) have borrowed many ideas developed in Pascal.

This book gives an informal introduction into the most important characteristics of Pascal, Modula, CHILL and Ada. Its authors are on the staff of a large electronic company: Philips. Expecting a rapid increase in the use of modern programming languages, Philips installed a 'Committee on Pascal-like languages' in January 1979 in order to be prepared for the ensuing demand for information and technical assistance. The primary task of this committee (usually called 'Pascal Group') is to give advice in the areas of modern programming languages, program development environments and software education. One of the projects of the Pascal Group was to provide the Philips software community with an introduction to four important modern languages: Pascal, Modula, CHILL and Ada. The resulting Philips report served as a basis for this book.

The languages will be discussed in historical order, one language per chapter. The book starts with an introductory chapter on some trends in programming language design and applications. Chapter 2 introduces the most important concepts in Pascal. In chapter 3 emphasis is put on those facilities in Modula which are not present in Pascal, i.e. concurrency and modules. An understanding of Pascal is required for the reading of this chapter. Chapters 4 and 5 introduce CHILL and Ada respectively. Again, the facilities which are either new or different from Pascal and Modula are emphasized. Both chapters can be read independently, but they refer frequently to Pascal and Modula.

For every language chapter, the first section discusses briefly the history, application area, standardization aspects and future prospects. Wherever appropriate, corresponding facilities in the languages are mentioned. Pascal, historically the first of the four, will be compared to

---

†Ada is a registered trademark of the US Government, Ada Joint Program Office

FORTRAN and RTL/2. The various language facilities are introduced through many examples. No judgement is given about the way the facilities are put in the overall structure of the language but sufficient background is given as to their use. Therefore this book can also be used as a first introduction into concepts like modules and abstract data types (3.5), concurrency (3.7, 3.8), exceptions (4.8, 5.8) and generics (5.10).

Throughout the book there has been an attempt to use a consistent terminology, even when the official language definitions use different terms for the same concept. This is done in order to avoid confusing the reader with new terms in every chapter. If possible, the same examples are shown in the different languages. This makes it easier for the reader to judge for himself how the various facilities can be expressed in the different languages.

It should be borne in mind that the primary purpose of this book is to give a concise and informal (but not imprecise) overview of facilities provided by the four languages. It is by no means a textbook for learning the details of a particular language.

There are at least three categories of readers that will find this book useful. In the first place, those who have some knowledge of high level programming languages based on older languages such as FORTRAN, ALGOL 60 or even Pascal and would like to extend their knowledge with concepts used in more recently developed programming languages. In the second place, those who have to choose a programming language for their applications, and want to be informed about the different capabilities of the languages. In the third place, computer science students who can use this book as a reference to the application of modern language design principles and programming concepts in some important actual programming languages.

A number of people have contributed in various ways to the present book. First of all we are indebted to the members of the Pascal Group for inspiring and encouraging our work. The Group consisted of – apart from the authors – R.H. Bourgonjon, J. van Eybergen, J.B. te Kiefte, F.E.J. Kruseman Aretz, H.C. de Ruyter van Steveninck, P.C.J. van Twist, B.L.A. Waumans and P. Wodon. All of them contributed in some form to the review of an earlier draft. In addition the following people have reviewed parts of the book: C. Breeus, R. Bruno, R.W.A.M.

Fabrie, P. Green, C. Hill, P. van Liere, A.C.M. Oerlemans, J. Rieske and L. Zigterman. Special thanks are due to F.E.J. Kruseman Aretz who took the trouble to review the whole book in considerable detail; his suggestions led to many improvements.

C.H. Smedema
P. Medema
M. Boasson

1 INTRODUCTION

1.1 TRENDS IN PROGRAMMING LANGUAGE DESIGN

Studies in the way programming languages are used (and misused) have led to a number of design considerations, of which some are listed below:

- The facilities of a language must be simple to understand in all situations where they can be used and free from unexpected interactions when they are combined (*clarity* and *orthogonality*).

- The notation (syntax) of the language must be easy to understand. The language shall aid the programmer in the design of his programs (*writeability*).

- The meaning of a program must be easily deducible from its text, without the excessive use of comments or other documentation (*readability*).

- It must be difficult to misuse the language (no tricks).

- Hierarchical or other modular design methods must be facilitated by providing suitable abstraction mechanisms in the language (e.g. procedure, module) and allowing proper control over the visibility of names.

- The language must be secure, i.e. all rules of the language shall be verifiable either by the compiler or during execution of the program.

The influence of these rules can be found in many places in the definition of Pascal and its descendent languages.

Programming languages in general are the result of the realization that abstraction is the most essential ingredient in programming. Every programming language more or less reflects the depth to which the understanding of the programming activity had evolved at the time of its conception. The structure of FORTRAN shows that emphasis is put on algorithms, especially on the separate actions to compose an algorithm: assignment, conditional- and loop statements. Data types are restricted to numeric purposes and the notion that properly used data types can make a program more readable and reliable is absent. ALGOL 60 is already better in several respects: it allows nested declarations and the type mechanism is much more secure.

A great deal of effort has since been devoted to ways describing not only the structure of algorithms, but also the structure of data. Pascal offers a nice - although not ideal - method to specify data and handle the associated data types. Note that Pascal is by no means the only language in this respect.

More problems were to come however. The size of the programs tended to grow beyond the limit where one human being could handle the entire program. Therefore, programs had to be split up in parts that could be designed and produced separately. Neither Pascal nor ALGOL 60 allows a program to be split up in parts. FORTRAN interestingly enough allows this, but no checks are done on the interfaces between the independently compiled parts.

Obviously more secure ways of handling this problem were needed. In addition the notion that data types are more than mere memory addresses began to gain widespread recognition. The term *abstract data type* was coined to indicate that data types consist of storage elements for data together with certain operations that are allowed on those data.

Many experimental languages were defined that implemented this concept of *abstract data type*: The definition of a data type is accompanied by the specification of the operations allowed on values of the type (often through procedures and functions). The language Modula uses the *module* for the specification of *abstract data types* as well as for the separate construction of program parts.

In large projects there is a need to protect programmers from inadvertently misusing implementation details which leads to programs that are difficult to modify because a modification in one module may have unforeseen effects on other modules. Therefore, the notion of information hiding, already at the basis of the abstract data type, has extended through the implementation of algorithms. Ada provides facilities to hide such implementation details from users of a given module.

New areas of programming activity have become the target of language designers: real-time systems have long remained the exclusive realm of assembly language programming. The main property of these systems is that several activities have to proceed in parallel. There is widespread agreement that this can be modelled in a programming language in terms of sequential *processes* each of which can proceed in parallel (also called: *concurrently*) with the others. The modern real-time languages (e.g. Modula, CHILL, Ada) all provide this process concept. However there is no agreement about how the cooperation between processes must be described; the various languages provide different mechanisms. Research continues in this area.

In programs that have to operate continuously in the presence of possible run-time errors, the traditional way of handling such errors cannot be used. It would be unacceptable e.g. if execution of a program controlling a telephone switching system were terminated in response to a run-time error "index out of bounds". Therefore a mechanism for specifying program execution in response to unforeseen conditions is essential. Both CHILL and Ada provide *exceptions* for this purpose.

The concept of generics represents a new level of abstraction. Modules that are different in the data types operated on but identical otherwise are regarded as parameterized instances of a (common) template. Ada includes facilities for the specification of generic program parts.

Finally it should be mentioned that, although all the concepts mentioned above are appealing, it is next to impossible to integrate them all in one properly designed programming language. This makes the modern real-time programming languages rather complex. A better understanding of the concepts and their relations may in the future lead to better, less complex programming languages.

1.2 TRENDS IN APPLICATIONS

The applications for which computers are being used have changed considerably over the past years. Hence the requirements for a programming language now are different from those of, say, 15 years ago.

Traditionally there were three distinct application areas:

- Solving numerical problems, with ALGOL 60 and FORTRAN as the major languages.

- Data processing, with COBOL as the most used language.

- Process Control (also called real-time or embedded computer systems) with often dedicated hardware programmed in assembly or machine languages.

Neither FORTRAN nor ALGOL 60 had data structuring facilities (apart from the array), while COBOL was inadequate for the writing of numerical algorithms. Later, languages for systems programming were designed, which included data structuring facilities, but without extensive format control for input/output operations and without floating point arithmetic for example. With the introduction of mini-computers, and, more recently, micro-computers, the field of embedded computer applications became rapidly more important. Higher level languages for these systems were introduced, but they were often only adaptations of existing languages (e.g. Real-Time FORTRAN).

It is becoming increasingly difficult to classify an application as "numerical", "data processing", or "embedded". Two or, often, all aspects are present in the application (e.g. in computer aided manufacturing). This makes the traditional languages inadequate for the problems of today.

1.3 TRENDS IN PROGRAMMING ENVIRONMENTS

For a few years it has been recognized that using a good programming language (and a good compiler for it) solves only some of the problems associated with making and maintaining a good quality software product.

During its life-time a software product passes through many phases: requirements specification, design, implementation, testing, production, and maintenance. The compiler helps only in the implementation phase. Some other tools useful in this phase are: a -preferably syntax oriented- editor, a pretty-printer, a tool for checking interfaces between separately compiled program units, and a data base of source and object programs with version control and configuration management.

Some other tools can be mentioned for the other phases. For testing, a suitable language oriented debugger is required. In the production phase a data base is needed for configuration and release control. In the maintenance phase, there must be facilities for complaint handling and change control. The tools for the design and requirements phase are still very much a research topic. A good programming language does help in the design.

An integrated set of tools as described above is called a programming environment, or a program development system. There are some environments available, but these are usually only for one language. Some implementations of an Ada programming environment have been started, and there are some projects on a common environment for Ada and CHILL.

1.4   OVERVIEW OF PASCAL, MODULA, CHILL AND ADA

Pascal is a language for sequential programming. It can be used for numerical applications as well as for the manipulation of many types of data. It has a well-structured set of control statements. It was designed in 1968 by Wirth of the Eidgenossische Technische Hochschule (ETH) in Zurich and it is widely used, in particular in universities. Recently the language also became popular in the industrial world, mainly because many microprocessor manufacturers, who did not have compatibility commitments and could choose the best language available, decided to use Pascal as their programming language. The International Standards Organization (ISO) has developed a Pascal standard, which became effective in 1982. It is expected that most Pascal implementations will adopt ISO Pascal as a kernel language. However, many extensions will be defined in the various implementations. There is no widespread agreement in this area.

Modula is a language for parallel programming and was also designed
by Wirth. He was especially concerned with an efficient implementation
for process control applications (also called real-time or embedded computer systems) on a one-processor machine. Modula programs can run
on minimal hardware, and do not require any operating system support
apart from a very small kernel. The sequential part of the language is a
subset of Pascal. Modula can play a significant role as a programming
language for small real-time systems. Because of its simplicity it is an
excellent tool to teach modern programming concepts. Based on his
experience with Modula, Wirth has designed another similar language
called Modula-2, which is now gaining more interest than its predecessor.

CHILL is a language for parallel programming on one-processor machines and distributed architectures. It was developed on request of the
CCITT (Comité Consultatif International Télégraphique et Téléphonique) by an international committee chaired by Bourgonjon (Philips'
Telecommunicatie Industrie, Hilversum). The final proposal was accepted by the CCITT's general assembly in 1980, and was called CHILL
(Ccitt HIgh Level Language). The language will have a major impact on
the programming of telecommunications systems in the world. Compilers are becoming available for special purpose as well as for com-
mercially available processors. The language is used by a number
of manufacturers of telecommunications switching systems. The sequential part of CHILL is based on Pascal. Constructs for parallel programming are partly derived from Modula, partly from other
sources. CHILL is a rather complex language, requiring a large compiler.

Ada is also a language for parallel programming, and designed for
both one-processor machines and distributed architectures. Its main
(initial) application area will be embedded computer systems. It has
been designed on request of the USA Department of Defense (DoD) and
its development has involved many contractors and consultants. The
final proposal was designed by a team led by Ichbiah of CII-Honeywell
Bull. It can be expected that Ada, because of the power of its sponsor,
will have a big impact on the programming culture in the world. In
1980 the initial definition was frozen and in 1982 the first experimental
implementation became available. Probably industrial use of Ada will
not start before 1985. The sequential part of the language is also
based on Pascal, but there are numerous deviations, and significant

extensions. The constructs for parallel programming look powerful, but there is little experience with their use. The language has many facilities, a voluminous description, and is rather complex. Its compilers will be large. The DoD does not want any subsetting of the language, but this may prove difficult to control.

As Ada and CHILL aim at similar application areas (telecommunications switching systems can be considered to belong to the general field of embedded computer systems) they have similar characteristics. Therefore in the near future there will certainly be competition between both languages. It is unlikely that this competition will eventually lead to one single language because of political differences.

2   PASCAL

2.1   INTRODUCTION

Pascal was designed by Wirth from the Eidgenossische Technische Hochschule (ETH), Zurich as a language to be used for his courses in programming. The language generated widespread interest, especially in university circles, because it was simple, easy to learn, it contained a well-structured set of control statements and a balanced set of facilities for numerical applications as well as for the manipulation of many types of data. A portable compiler was available, so that implementing it on a new computer was rather simple and cheap. This was of great help spreading Pascal in the university world, and beyond.

For a number of years the large computer manufacturers did not show any interest. With the introduction of micro-computers a number of new companies (often originating from the semiconductor industry) started to manufacture small computers. Several factors have contributed to the rapid increase in popularity of Pascal on these small systems:

• The new companies had no previous investments in large software projects written in other languages, and compatibility requirements were of no concern to them. They were in a position to choose the best language available.

• Recent graduates from computer-science departments of universities often obtained responsible positions in these new companies. They took the opportunity to implement the language they had learned at the university.

• The University of California in San Diego (UCSD) adapted the original portable Pascal compiler such that it could run on a microprocessor-based system. They also wrote an operating system in Pascal, which included a good screen-oriented editor. Compiler plus operating system was easily transportable to new hardware and this contributed considerably to the success of the UCSD Pascal†.   It is now available on many different

---

†trademark of the Regents of the University of California

microprocessor configurations.

* There was a broad user-base available, consisting of recent graduates, who were able to persuade their management to acquire
  a small computer system with Pascal.

Pascal in those days had many aspects of an underground movement,
where users and small computer manufacturers joined forces. Later on
the movement also obtained support from computer hobbyists.

The large computer manufacturers were still not interested. One of
the reasons was the absence of an internationally accepted standard.
The original Pascal definition included ambiguities which had led to
different interpretations of the language. Moreover people started to
extend Pascal in different ways. This probably scared off the large
computer manufacturers.

The ISO standardization process for Pascal is now finished. Fortunately
there was widespread international agreement about the non-extended
kernel of the language. The member countries of the ISO have accepted
the Pascal standard of the British Standards Institute. Current implementations of Pascal will probably be changed such that ISO-Pascal
is offered as a proper subset. Most large computer manufacturers now
offer Pascal as a standard product. Within ANSI there is a group working on standardization of extensions to Pascal. It will be rather difficult
to reach agreement in this area.

The most important characteristics will be briefly introduced in the
next sections. Emphasis will be put on the concept of "type", as this
is one of the major differences between Pascal and older languages like
FORTRAN.

2.2   TYPES

2.2.1   Introduction

In Pascal every variable must be declared to be of a certain type. The
type defines the set of values that the variable may assume, and the
valid operations on these values. This type may be either one of the
predefined simple types: *real, integer, boolean, char* or it may be a user
defined type. User defined types can be simple types (enumeration types
and subrange types), structured types, or pointer types. Simple types
excluding the type *real* are called "discrete types".

Generally, operations on values of different type are not allowed. This
can be checked by the compiler. Provided that the programmer care-
fully chooses the types of his variables from the wide variety of types
available in Pascal, a Pascal-compiler can detect many more errors in
a program than a compiler for a language in which the type concept
does not play such an important role.

Some examples of type definitions and variable declarations are given
below. In many subsequent examples of Pascal, and also of Modula,
CHILL and Ada, these types and variables will be used. Hence this list
serves as a reference for the entire document and should be consulted
whenever type- or variable names are used in an example, without being
defined in, or immediately before that example.

All of the type definitions below will be introduced in the following
sections.

    type *day* = *(mon, tues, wed, thur, fri, sat, sun)* ;
         visa = *(permanent, temporary, visiting)* ;
         workday = *mon..fri* ;
         index = *first..last* ;
         years = *0..old* ;
         words = **packed array** *[index]* **of** *char* ;
         workweek = **array** *[workday]* **of** *boolean* ;
         wdayset = **set of** *workday* ;

```
person =
  record
    name : words ;
    age : years ;
    present : workweek ;
    citizen : boolean
  end ;
people = array [1..max] of person ;
list = file of person ;
reftoperson = ↑person ;
newperson =
  record
    name : words ;
    age : years ;
    present : workweek ;
    case citizen : boolean of
      true : (pensionno : integer) ;
      false : (status : visa; passportno: integer)
  end ;
chainperson =
  record
    human : person ;
    next : linktoperson
  end ;
linktoperson = ↑chainperson ;
```

Some examples of variable declarations are:

```
var counter : integer ;
    cross, dollar, percent, vacation : boolean ;
    sign, digit, nodigit : boolean ;
    i : index ;
    d1, d2 : day ;
    command : words ;
    firstweek : workweek ;
    week1, week2 : wdayset ;
    johnson, harris, someperson : person ;
    employees : list ;
    p, q : reftoperson ;
    ferguson, smith : newperson ;
    head, current : linktoperson ;
```

2.2.2   Constant definitions

With a constant definition it is possible to introduce a name as a
synonym for a constant of a predefined simple type (*integer, boolean,
char, real*). Also string-constants (a string is an array of char) can be
defined. Some examples are:

   const *first = 1 ; last = 9 ;*
      old = 110 ;
      max = 100 ;
      yell = 'I Like Pascal' ;

The use of names for constants makes a program more readable. It
also allows the parametrization (and hence the portability) of programs
and procedures: when the constant definitions are conveniently grouped
they can easily be recognized and changed to tune a program (or
procedure) to a particular application or machine.

2.2.3   Enumeration Types

Enumeration types enable the definition of simple user-defined types
by enumerating the identifiers which denote the values of the type, for
example:

   type *switch = (off, half, full) ;*
   var *sw : switch ;*

The variable *sw* of type *switch* can only assume the values *off, half* and
full. Hence statements like:

   sw := 1 ;
   if *sw = mon* **then** ...

are forbidden (this can be checked by the compiler) and statements
like:

   sw := off ;
   if *sw = full* **then** *sw := half ;*

are allowed.

In languages like FORTRAN and RTL/2 the constants *off*, *half* and *full* have to be mapped on the type integer. For example in FORTRAN we would have to declare:

INTEGER SWF

Among the range of integer values we have to choose three to represent the positions of the switch, e.g. *0* for *off*, *1* for *half* and *2* for *full*. However an assignment like

SWF = 100

is a correct FORTRAN assignment although it does not denote a switch position and it could produce erroneous results.

Enumeration types make it possible for the compiler to check against inconsistent use and incompatible operations (e.g. arithmetic operations on *sw*). The use of suggestive names for the constants of an enumeration type is very helpful when designing the program and improves its readability considerably.

There is an internal ordering assumed among the constants of an enumeration type. This allows the use of relational operators with enumeration types. For example let

type *day = (mon, tues, wed, thur, fri, sat, sun)* ;
var *d1, d2 : day* ;

then the following statements are allowed:

if *d1 < d2* **then** *sw := off* ;
if *d2 > wed* **then** *d1 := mon* **else** *d1 := sat* ;

On all values (or expressions) of a discrete type the operations *succ* and *pred* can be applied, which give the successor and predecessor values respectively (if they exist). For example, assuming that *d1* contains the value *tues*, *wed* will be assigned to *d2* in the following statement:

d2 := succ(d1) ;

2.2.4   Subrange Types

Subranges of already defined discrete types may be specified by giving
the lower and upper bounds of the subrange, for example:

type *workday* = *mon..fri ;*
   index = *first..last ;*
   years = *0..old ;*

In this way the range of values can be restricted. For example the
variable *i* declared by

   var *i : index ;*

can only assume integer values in the range *first* to *last* (i.e. 1 to 9
according to the **const** definition of section 2.2.2).

The compiler may use the information to economize on storage. At run-
time and sometimes at compile-time, violations of the range restriction
can be checked.

2.2.5   Structured Types

Types with more than one component are called structured types.
Pascal has the array, record, file and set types. These give Pascal much
better facilities for data structuring than e.g. FORTRAN (only array)
and RTL/2 (only array and record). Moreover in RTL/2 structured
variables and types can only be declared globally. In Pascal however
they can be declared locally inside procedures and functions (like any
other type or variable, see section 2.4).

In a type definition it is possible to specify that a structured type must
be packed. This is an indication for the compiler that it may economize
on storage, possibly at the expense of access efficiency. There are also
predefined procedures which cause (un)packing of arrays.

2.2.6   Array Types

In an array all components are of the same type. The index type can
be any discrete type, i.e. (subrange of) *integer, boolean, char*, and
enumeration. The array has one component for each value in the index
type. The components can be selected by the use of subscripts. For
example:

> **type** *workweek* = **array** *[workday]* **of** *boolean ;*
> *letterfreq* = **array** *['A'..'Z']* **of** *integer ;*

Assuming:

> **var** *firstweek : workweek ;*
> *alphabet : letterfreq ;*

possible assignments are:

> *firstweek[mon] :=* *false ;*
> *alphabet ['Q'] :=* *10 ;*

Arrays can have any number of dimensions.

Strings in Pascal can be handled with the type "packed array of char",
for example:

> **type** *words* = **packed array** *[index]* **of** *char ;*
> **var** *command : words ;*

Some possible statements are:

> *command :=* *'switch on' ;*
> *command[i+2] :=* *' ' ;*

Pascal does not include special facilities for handling strings, apart from
the possibility to make string-values by enclosing characters between
quotes.

2.2.7   Record Types

A record can contain components of different types, for example:

```
type person =
  record
    name : words ;
    age : years ;
    present : workweek ;
    citizen : boolean
  end ;
```

Variables of type *person* can be declared, for example:

```
var johnson, harris : person ;
```

The components of a record are called fields. They can be accessed by appending the fieldname (in this case *name, age, present,* or *citizen*) to the name of the record, separated by a dot. Some examples of assignments to record fields are:

```
johnson.age := 43 ;
harris.present[tues] := true ;
```

A record may contain a so-called variant part, which follows the fixed part. For example, depending on the citizenship it may be required to have fields containing different information. In this case the field *citizen* is used as selector (also called: "tag field") of the variant part:

```
type visa = (permanent, temporary, visiting) ;
  newperson =
    record
      name : words ;
      age : years ;
      present : workweek ;
    case citizen : boolean of
      true : (pensionno : integer) ;
      false : (status : visa; passportno: integer)
    end ;
```

This record type contains the same four fixed fields as in the type *person*. The fixed field *citizen* is the tag field, and it is enclosed by **case..of**. The variant part in this example has two alternatives. The tag field determines the existence of either a group containing the field *pensionno* or a group containing the fields *status* and *passportno*. Assuming

var *ferguson, smith* : *newperson ;*

some assignments to record-fields are:

ferguson. citizen := *false ;*
ferguson. status := *visiting ;*
smith. citizen := *true ;*
smith. pensionno := *23619 ;*

However,

smith. passportno := *87431 ;*

would now be illegal, because the tag field of *smith* has been given the value *true*, and consequently this variant does not exist for *smith*.

RTL/2 does not allow variant parts in record definitions.

2.2.8   Set Types

A set is an (unordered) collection of elements of the same (discrete) type. For example:

type *wdayset* = **set of** *workday ;*
var *week1, week2* : *wdayset ;*

The variables *week1* and *week2* may contain elements of type *workday*. The maximum number of elements is determined by the element-type (in the case of *workday* it is 5) and the minimum is no element at all (empty). Examples of assigning set-values to set-variables are:

week1 := *[mon, tues, fri] ;*
week2 := *[tues, wed] ;*

After the assignments the variable *week1* is the set which contains the elements *mon, tues* and *fri*, while *week2* contains *tues* and *wed*. Operations on values of type set are union, intersection, and set-difference:

- Union (+), e.g. week1 + week2 contains all elements which are element of *week1* or *week2* or both, i.e. *mon, tues, wed* and *fri*.

- Intersection (*), e.g. week1 * week2 contains all elements which
  are both element of *week1* and *week2*, i.e. *tues.*

- Difference (−), e.g. week1 − week2 contains all elements of
  week1 that are not also elements of *week2*, i.e. *mon* and *fri.*

It is also possible to compare two sets (whether they contain the same
elements) and to test set inclusion (whether all elements of one set
are also elements of another set). Finally there is a membership test
(whether a set contains a specified element). As an example of the
membership test, consider the following statement:

  if *(d1=mon)* **or** *(d1=tues)* **or** *(d1=wed)* **or** *(d1=fri)* **then** ..

Using the set-membership test this becomes:

  if *d1* **in** *[mon..wed, fri]* **then** . .

Sets are very important in systems programming. When they are not
provided by the language (neither FORTRAN nor RTL/2 have sets)
they have to be programmed, e.g. using arrays of boolean values.
This is not only rather inefficient (sets are usually implemented with
bitstrings and operations on sets can be performed by logical machine
instructions) but it also obscures the program. As an example consider
the field *present* in the record-type *person.* Assume that we want to
know on which days both *johnson* and *harris* are present. Since *present*
is defined as a boolean array, a loop has to be programmed which
performs a logical **and** operation on all elements of the array. However,
present could also have been defined as a set:

  type *person* =
    record
      name : words ;
      age : years ;
      present : wdayset ;
      citizen : boolean
    end ;

Assuming

  var *result : wdayset ;*

the solution to the problem would have been very simple and clear:

result := johnson.present * harris.present ;

2.2.9   File Types

In Pascal sequential files can be defined, for example:

type *list* = **file of** *person ;*

An existing file can be initialized for reading with the predefined procedure *reset* and subsequent elements can be read by calling the predefined procedure *read.* For example, assuming

var *counter : integer ;*
  someperson : person ;
  employees : list ;

the following program section counts the number of persons who are citizen in the file *employees:*

reset (employees) ;
counter := 0 ;
while not *eof (employees)* **do**
begin
  read (employees, someperson) ;
  if *someperson.citizen* **then** *counter := counter + 1*
end ;

A file can be made empty using the predefined procedure *rewrite* and elements can be appended to the file by calling the procedure *write,* for example:

rewrite (employees) ;
write (employees, johnson) ;
write (employees, harris) ;

Although it is nowhere stated in the Pascal definition, files are implemented by storing them on some external device, for example disks. They are also used to interface Pascal to external file systems. There exist a predefined file type *text* and two predefined files of type *text,* called *input* and *output,* through which input/output to text oriented devices can take place. Formatting information for text files can be given via additional parameters in the procedures *read* and *write*.

In RTL/2 and FORTRAN there is no file type. Input/output to files on e.g. disks is possible, but type checking can not be done, and the file type remains invisible to the user.

Many Pascal implementations have different extensions and/or restrictions to the file type because the concept of a file type interacts very closely with the underlying operating system. Some implementations have extended the operations on files with random access to elements in a file.

2.2.10   Pointer Types

It is possible to dynamically create (i.e. during program execution) new variables. As their addresses can not be determined at compile-time, these variables are accessed via pointers (also called: references). For example

    type *reftoperson* $= \uparrow person$;

introduces a pointer type named *reftoperson* whose values are pointers (indicated by $\uparrow$) to dynamically allocated variables of type *person*. The declaration

    var *p, q : reftoperson* ;

introduces two variables, *p* and *q*, which are potential pointers to objects of type *person* (and cannot be used to point to objects of any other type). Dynamic variables can only be created by calling the standard procedure *new*, for example:

    new(p) ;

A new variable of type *person* has now been created and *p* is made to refer to it. The variable itself can be accessed via *dereferencing* of the pointer *p*. This is denoted by *p*$\uparrow$. The fields of the newly created record variable can for example be initialized as follows:

    p$\uparrow$*.citizen :*$=$ *false* ;
    p$\uparrow$*.age :*$=$ *38* ;

Pointers can be assigned to other pointers, for example after

$q := p$;

the same person can be accessed via the pointer variables p and q. The value **nil** can be assigned to any pointer to indicate that this pointer is currently not referring to a (dynamically created) variable, for example:

$q := nil$;

Storage for dynamically created variables can be released by calling the standard procedure *dispose*, for example

dispose (p) ;

With pointer types complex data structures can be built dynamically, e.g. linked lists. As an example consider a record type definition with two fields, one containing a field of type *person* and the second containing a field with a type: pointer to its own type. This can be defined with the following two type definitions:

```
type linktoperson = ↑ chainperson ;
   chainperson =
     record
       human : person ;
       next : linktoperson
     end ;
var head, current : linktoperson ;
```

A linked list can be made by repeating the following statements (assuming *head* contains **nil** initially):

```
new (current) ;
current ↑.next := head ;
head := current ;
```

The dynamic creation of variables is not possible in FORTRAN or RTL/2. RTL/2 however (unlike Pascal), allows pointers to refer to static variables.

2.3 STATEMENTS

Pascal contains a simple and well structured set of conditional- and loop statements.

The conditional statements are the **if** statement (with an optional **else** part) and the **case** statement (a multiway switch). For example:

```
if johnson.present[mon]
    then begin
        week1 := week1 + [mon] ;
        counter := counter + 1
    end
    else vacation := true ;

case command[i] of
    ' # ' : cross := true ;
    ' $ ' : dollar := true ;
    '%' : percent := true
end ;
```

Unlike FORTRAN, the conditional execution of statements in Pascal (usually) does not require the use of **goto** statements. Thus users have facilities that do not obscure the flow of control in their program.

Note that the two statements after **then** are enclosed by **begin..end**. In Pascal there is only one statement allowed in the **then** and **else** parts of an **if** statement (this applies also to loop statements, except for **repeat..until** and the **with** statement. See below). When more statements are needed, they have to be enclosed by **begin..end**, thus forming one so-called compound statement.

Pascal has three loop constructs 1) the **for** loop, 2) the **while** loop (which tests a condition at the beginning of the loop) and 3) the **repeat..until** loop (which has the test at the end of the loop). The latter two loop constructs facilitate the writing of programs with a much better structure than is possible in FORTRAN, where often a **goto** statement has to be used to exit from a loop on a certain condition. RTL/2 has a **while**-loop, but no **repeat..until**-loop. Some examples:

```
while (command[i] <> ' ') and (i <= 5) do
  begin
    command[i] := '$' ;
    i := i + 1
  end ;

current := head ;
while current <> nil do
  begin
    . . . .
    current := current ↑.next
  end ;

repeat i := i + 1 until command[i] <> '$' ;

for d1 := mon to fri do firstweek[d1] := true ;
```

Pascal has a so-called **with** statement, which allows access to fields of
a record without having to use the record variable name, for example:

```
with harris do
  begin
    name : = 'Harris   ' ;
    age := 23 ;
    for d1 := mon to fri do present[d1] := true ;
    citizen := true
  end ;
```

2.4 SUBPROGRAMS

Subprograms in Pascal are 1) the procedure and 2) the function. They
are similar to procedures and functions in RTL/2 and ALGOL 60. The
execution of a procedure is started by a procedure call statement, while
the execution of a function is started by encountering its name during
the evaluation of an expression. A function delivers a value as a result
of its execution.

Subprograms have to be declared. The declaration consists of a heading
and a body. The heading specifies whether it is a procedure or a
function, the name of the subprogram, the names and types of the
so-called formal parameters and, in case of a function, the type of

the result (which must be a simple type). An example of a procedure declaration is (comments are enclosed by *(* and *)*):

```
(* heading *)
procedure chop ( var left : integer; limit : integer) ;
(* body *)
begin
   if left > limit then left := limit
end ;
```

The procedure's name is *chop*, the names of the formal parameters are *left* and *limit*, and their type is *integer*.

Before the subprogram is executed, the so-called actual parameters must be supplied. The types of the actual parameters must correspond with the types of the formal parameters (the ISO-Pascal definition specifies what *correspond* means). As an example assume:

```
var x : integer ;
x := 15 ;
```

then the following procedure call statement causes the execution of the procedure *chop*:

```
chop (x,10) ;
```

The actual parameters are x and *10*.

Formal parameters can be specified as so-called value parameters or as variable parameters. This distinction determines the way the actual parameters are associated with the formal parameters. In the procedure heading, formal variable parameters are preceded by the keyword **var**. In the above example, *left* is a formal variable parameter while *limit* is a formal value parameter.

Formal value parameters can be considered as local variables of the subprogram. Before the actual execution of the body of the subprogram starts, the values of the actual value parameters (*10* in this case) are copied into the formal value parameters (*limit*). Nothing else happens, hence values passed by value parameters can be considered as input to the subprogram. Results of the execution of the subprogram can never be passed through value parameters.

For formal variable parameters, accessing the formal parameter (*left* in this case) during the execution of the subprogram means in fact accessing the actual variable parameter (*x*) directly. Since *x* is declared outside the procedure body, results of a subprogram execution can be transferred through variable parameters. Note that the subprogram can also make use of any value which an actual variable parameter may have prior to the execution of the subprogram. Hence variable parameters can be used for input as well as for output. This is actually used in this example: the value contained in *x* is first inspected, and then modified in case it exceeds *limit*. After execution of the procedure call statement, *x* contains *10*.

Assuming:

var *y : integer ;*
y := 6 ;

the procedure call statement

chop (x,y) ;

is also possible, because *x* is a variable and *y* delivers an integer value (*6*). However the procedure call

chop (10,y) ;

would be illegal, because *10* is not a variable.

Variable parameters are also called reference parameters. Associating actual parameters with formal parameters is also called *parameter passing by reference* in case of variable parameters and *parameter passing by value* in case of value parameters.

As an example of a function using value parameters consider:

function *older (p1, p2 : person) : boolean ;*
begin
    older := p1.age > p2.age
end ;

An example of its use is:

if *older (harris, johnson)* **then** . . . .

p1 and *p2* are the formal value parameters, while *harris* and *johnson* are the actual value parameters. The function delivers a value of *boolean* type as result.

Every subprogram declaration defines a new scope. Within a subprogram local variables, types, constants and other subprograms can be defined. Their names are invisible outside the subprogram. Local variables only exist during the execution of the subprogram.

On the other hand, names defined outside the subprogram are visible inside the subprogram, provided the same name is not redefined inside the subprogram. Names defined outside the subprogram are called global to that subprogram. Hence it is possible to access global variables from within a subprogram and results of a subprogram execution may be returned through changing the values of global variables.

As an example consider the following procedure declaration which, after incrementing the age of all persons in an array of persons, counts the number of adults (age > 20):

```
(* global declarations and definitions *)
const max = 100 ;
type people = array [1..max] of person ;
var counter : integer ;

(* procedure declaration *)
(* heading *)
procedure countadult ( var p : people) ;
(* body *)
(* local declaration *)
var i : 1..max ;
(* statement part *)
begin
  for i := 1 to max do
    with p[i] do
      begin
        if age < old then age := age + 1 ;
        if age > 20 then counter := counter + 1
      end
end ;
```

Assuming the declaration

var *league1, league2 : people ;*

the procedure could be called as follows:

countadult (league1) ; countadult (league2) ;

In this case *p* is a formal variable parameter, because it is preceded by **var** in the procedure heading. The actual parameters (which must be variables) *league1* and *league2* will be accessed whenever the formal parameter *p* is used in the procedure declaration. Hence *p[i].age* directly refers to the field *age* of the actual parameter (*league1* or *league2*).

The result of this procedure is not returned via another variable parameter (which could have been done) but it is accumulated in the global variable *counter*. After the above two calls to *countadult*, this variable contains the total number of adults in *league1* and *league2*. Note that *counter* should be initialized before calling *countadult*.

The variable *i* is a local variable of the procedure *countadult* and is not visible outside the procedure. In other words the scope of the variable *i* is the procedure *countadult* because only within this procedure the name *i* can be used with the meaning as declared.

The procedure *countadult* as defined above always requires an actual array parameter of type *people*, with index bounds *1* and *max*. The value of *max* must be made equivalent to some integer value in a constant definition. Hence this value is fixed in the program, and *countadult* cannot be called with an array with different bounds. This is a severe restriction, which was present in Pascal as defined originally by Wirth. However ISO Pascal allows flexible array bounds for formal parameters. For example the same procedure *countadult* can be written as follows:

```
procedure countadult2 ( var p : array [lo..hi : integer] of person) ;
   var i: integer ;
begin
   for i := lo to hi do
      with p[i] do
         begin
            if age < old then age := age + 1 ;
```

$$\textbf{if } \textit{age} > \textit{20} \textbf{ then } \textit{counter} := \textit{counter} + \textit{1}$$
$$\textbf{end}$$
$$\textbf{end } ;$$

p is called a conformant array parameter and lo and hi are the (formal) index bounds of the array. The procedure *countadult2* can be called with any size of array of *person*. The actual array bounds are assigned to lo and hi when the procedure is called.

In Pascal a formal parameter can also be a subprogram. Recursive subprogram calls are allowed.

In FORTRAN, parameter passing is always by reference and recursive subprogram calls are not allowed. In RTL/2, variables of array and record type may not be declared as local variables within a subprogram.

The order of declarations and definitions in a subprogram is always:

- constant definitions

- type definitions

- variable declarations

- (local) subprogram declarations

- statements

This holds also for the main program at the outermost level, which is in fact a procedure with the keyword **procedure** replaced by **program**. The general rule is that names can only be used after they have been defined. However, there are a few exceptions for pointers and subprograms.

2.5   PASCAL EXTENSIONS

The growing popularity of Pascal, added to the fact that other adequate languages were not easily available, stimulated the use of Pascal in application fields for which it was not originally intended. This caused some criticism on the limited facilities of Pascal and many application-specific extensions to Pascal were introduced. The main points of criticism from the different application areas can be summarized as follows:

numerical:

- No exponentiation operator (there is a standard function *exp*).

- No provision for single and double length arithmetic.

- No variable array bounds (problem partly solved by conformant array parameters in ISO Pascal).

data processing:

- No long decimal constants.

- String handling too limited.

- No random access files.

operating systems and embedded computer systems:

- No concurrency.

- No control over low level input/output and interrupts.

Therefore most Pascal implementations support more then ISO Pascal. Some of the most popular extensions are:

- Single and double precision *integer* and/or *real* types.

- Exponentiation operator.

- Manipulations for strings of dynamic length.

- Initialization of variables in a so-called **value** declaration.

- Functions may return not only simple types, but also structured types (except the *file* type).

- Constant definitions not only for simple types and strings, but also for structured types. The **with** statement can be used for accessing fields in these structured constants.

- Constant expressions allowed in many cases where ISO Pascal requires a constant.

- Subranges allowed in labels used in the variant part of a record and in the **case** statement.

- **otherwise** clause in **case** statement.

- **exit** statement to allow "controlled" conditional exit of a subprogram and a loop.

- **assert** statement to check a specified condition at execution of the program.

- Facilities for separate compilation.

- Facilities to handle "external files" within a Pascal program, and random access of files.

Many of the above mentioned extensions have been included in subsequently developed programming languages, like Modula, CHILL and Ada. Within the ANSI (American National Standards Institute) there is a committee dealing with the standardization of a few extensions to ISO Pascal. However there is widespread disagreement about which extensions to standardize and in which way.

ISO Pascal is different from Pascal as defined by Wirth in two major aspects: the specification of formal subprogram parameters has been enhanced (to allow type-checking) and the so-called conformant array parameters have been added (to allow flexible array bounds for formal parameters). ISO Pascal allows two levels of compliance: level 0 without conformant array parameters, and level 1 with conformant array parameters.

It can be expected that eventually all major Pascal implementations will have ISO Pascal as a proper subset. Most implementations have a switch which can turn on an ISO Pascal mode, which means that all constructs not part of ISO Pascal are flagged.

2.6 PASCAL DESCENDANTS

Operating systems and real-time (also called embedded computer) systems are usually programmed as a collection of cooperating concurrent processes which are synchronized with each other by (software) signals, and with the external world by (hardware) interrupts. Each process is a "normal" sequential program.

When the manufacturers of micro-computers and micro-processor development systems turned to Pascal, they discovered after some time that Pascal is not suitable for programming operating systems and real-time systems. However, this application area was rather important for them. Rather than turning to more suitable language definitions (which were available, see below) they extended Pascal in order to profit from Pascal's popularity. The main extensions are:

- The possibility to define a process, which can run concurrently with other processes in the system.

- Synchronization between processes is often done with software signals called *semaphores*.

- Interrupts can be translated into semaphores, so that a process can be synchronized with external hardware.

- Addresses for variables and semaphores can be specified (e.g. for interrupt vector locations or input/output ports).

As has been mentioned already, several programming languages for real-time and operating systems applications have been defined. The following is a -not exhaustive- list of Pascal-based languages, i.e. in the sequential part of the language definition there is at least some Pascal influence :

- Concurrent Pascal (Brinch Hansen, California Institute of Technology, 1974)

- Modula (Wirth, ETH, Zurich, 1976)

- Modula-2 (Wirth, ETH, Zurich, 1978)

- Portal (Landis and Gyr, Zug / ETH, Zurich, 1978)

- Pascal-plus (Hoare, Queen's University, Belfast, 1978)

- CHILL (CCITT, 1980)

- Ada (US Government, 1983)

Concurrent Pascal, Modula, Modula-2 and Pascal-plus all originate from universities. Only a few commercial implementations are available, and their use is largely restricted to universities and research institutes. Modula-2 certainly has the potential of spreading to a larger user community. Portal was a joint development of the Swiss-based company Landis and Gyr and the Eidgenossische Technische Hochschule, Zurich. It is used as an in-house language.

CHILL and Ada are recent developments of very important user-groups: telecommunication and defense. Because of their application areas and the power of their supporting organizations these languages will become very important in the near future. Their definitions will be discussed in the next chapters. However first the language Modula will be presented, because several new concepts in Modula have influenced both CHILL and Ada.

3 MODULA

3.1 INTRODUCTION

Modula was designed by Wirth for the programming of real-time systems. He gives two requirements for languages in this area:

- Facilities to program concurrent execution of several activities (e.g. several physical quantities have to be monitored at different frequencies).

- Facilities to program input/output operations to any device (i.e. not only to standard devices like visual display unit, printer, disc, etc., but also to e.g. analog-to-digital-converter, external timer).

Because of the first requirement Modula has the facility to specify a piece of program as a *process* which can be executed in parallel (also called: concurrently) with other processes in the system. These processes can communicate with each other via shared variables declared in *interface modules*.

The second requirement cannot be solved in a machine-independent way, but Modula isolates the machine-dependent parts of a program (e.g. interrupt- and priority structure) in *device modules*. Within device modules, machine registers and addresses can be associated with variable names. There is no need to resort to assembly language programming, even when input/output operations are time-critical (provided the implementation is done in an efficient way).

Modula derives its name from a new concept in the language : a *module*. A module allows precise control over the visibility of names and provides a powerful mechanism to introduce new types. Moreover, with modules it is possible to provide a secure facility for separate compilation. In Pascal this is not possible. Both Ada and CHILL provide facilities comparable to modules.

Facilities for high-level input/output (e.g. reading from and writing to files) are not included in the language because they can be programmed

in the language itself. Modula programs are meant to be executed on
an almost "bare" computer (i.e. without a large operating system).
Only a small kernel operating system (written in the language of the
target machine) of about 400 bytes is required. This makes Modula
especially suitable for small real-time systems.

Modula is not a wide-spread language. A few compilers are available.
Most users of Modula can be found in universities and research institutes. Modula to some extent influenced later languages like Ada
and CHILL.

Wirth has developed another language which he called Modula-2. The
facilities for concurrent programming in Modula-2 are more primitive,
and hence more flexible than in Modula. This makes Modula-2 especially suitable as a systems programming language, while Modula is
more a language for real-time applications with higher level facilities
for controlling concurrent actions. On the other hand it is relatively
straightforward to write Modula's facilities for concurrency with the
primitives that Modula-2 provides. Modula-2 is now gaining popularity
and compilers are available as commercial products.

When designing Modula, Wirth had a one-processor machine in mind.
Using it for distributed target architectures is in principle possible,
but not convenient. Modula-2 was specifically designed for a single
processor machine, and it cannot be used on distributed architectures.
In section 3.9 the main differences between Modula and Modula-2 are
briefly listed.

Compared to Ada and CHILL, Modula is much simpler, easier to
learn, has less facilities (e.g. no exception handling) and requires a
much smaller compiler. This makes Modula especially suitable as a
language for small embedded systems. Its simple structure provides
a good opportunity to become familiar with the concepts of modules
and concurrency, without the burden of learning a large and complex
language. From a technical point of view it would be much better
for (micro)processor development systems to offer Modula or Modula-2,
rather than Pascal with a number of ad-hoc extensions, because:

• The concurrency facilities are integrated into the language.

• Device communication is integrated into the language.

- Modules provide, apart from other facilities, the "natural" units for separate compilation.

- Only a very small kernel operating system is required in the target processor.

- Further operating system facilities can be written in the language itself, thus facilitating portability to other processors.

Modula can be divided into three parts:

- The sequential part, which is derived from Pascal. The most important addition is the concept of a *module* (sections 3.2 to 3.5).

- The machine-independent parallel part, with the notions of *process, interface module* and *signal* (sections 3.6, 3.7).

- The machine-dependent part, with the notions of *device module* and *device process* (section 3.8).

3.2 TYPES

Modula has four predefined simple types (compare Pascal section 2.2.1): *integer, boolean, character* and *bits*. There is no *real* type because Wirth did not consider it essential for systems programming. Modula-2 includes the *real* type.

The *bits* type can be considered as an array of boolean, where the wordlength of the machine is the size of the array. It is a simple replacement for the set type of Pascal (section 2.2.8), which is not available in Modula. Applicable operators on values of *bits* type are: **and, or, xor, not** and comparison for (in)equality. The way in which values of *bits* type are written is reminiscent of the set values in Pascal. Assuming the following variable declaration:

var *state, mask : bits ;*

some possible assignments for an implementation with a 16-bit word-length are (index runs from 0 to 15, comments in Modula are enclosed between *(** and **)*):

mask := *[2:5, 7]* ;
(* bits 2,3,4,5 and 7 are set true, the others false *)
state := *mask* and *[4, 7:11]* ;
(* bits 4 and 7 become true *)

Other simple types can be defined by enumeration, as in Pascal (section 2.2.3). Modula has no subrange types.

The structured types in Modula are the **array** and the **record** (without variants). Arrays have a slightly different syntax from Pascal. The upper and lower bounds of the array in a type definition must always be mentioned explicitly, because Modula has no subrange types. For example (compare with section 2.2.6):

  type *words* = **array** *first : last* **of** *char* ;
  workweek = **array** *mon : fri* **of** *boolean* ;

The file type is absent (because files and operations on files can be implemented in Modula according to the user's wishes) as are the set type and the pointer type.

In Modula, Wirth has minimized the language in order to make it simple. He was probably too drastic, because in Modula-2 he has brought back all the types of Pascal, except for files (see 3.9).

3.3 STATEMENTS

In Pascal only one statement can conditionally be executed in an **if** statement. Similarly a **for** statement, a **while** statement and a **with** statement can only contain one statement. When the execution of more statements is required, they have to be enclosed by **begin** and **end**, to form one compound statement. For example (see section 2.3):

  while *i* <= *5* **do** *i* := *i* + *1* ;

  while *i* <= *5* **do** **begin** *command[i]*:= *'$'*; *i*:= *i+1* **end** ;

This means that insertion or deletion of one statement may require insertion or deletion of the symbols **begin**..**end** (similar to ALGOL 60).

In Modula the loop- and conditional statements (except **repeat..until**) always close with the symbol **end**, which results in a more uniform appearance of statements in all situations. For example:

while $i <= 5$ **do** $i := i + 1$ **end** ;

while $i <= 5$ **do** *command[i]* := '$'; $i := i + 1$ **end** ;

In Ada and CHILL control statements are also closed with an explicit symbol; however each statement type has a unique closing symbol.

Conditional statements in Modula are the **if**- and the **case** statement (similar to Pascal). The **if** statement contains an optional **elsif**-part, which is used if several conditions have to be checked sequentially. This saves a number of closing **end** symbols and makes the program more readable. For example:

if *command[i]* $=$ '#'
  then *cross* := *true*
elsif *(command[i]* $=$ '$') **and** $(i = 3)$
  then *dollar* := *true*
  else *percent* := *true*
end ;

Modula has three loop constructs: the **while** statement, the **repeat** statement and a general **loop** statement. The latter statement is a kind of substitute for the **for**- and **goto** statements, which are both absent in Modula. The **loop** statement specifies a loop which can be conditionally terminated at any point. For example:

loop
  when $i >$ *last* **exit**
  when *command[i]* $=$ '#' **do** *cross* := *true* **exit**
  when *command[i]* $=$ '$' **do** *dollar* := *true* **exit**
  $i := i + 1$
end ;

If a **when**-clause is encountered, its condition is evaluated and when it yields true, the statement(s) after **do** are executed (if any) and the loop is terminated. Otherwise the next statement is executed (which may be any statement or another **when**-clause). When the end of the loop is reached (i.e. all conditions were false) the first statement of the loop is executed again. All repetitions can be expressed by **loop** statements and the **while-** and **repeat** statements merely express simple and frequently occurring cases. Processes in real-time systems and operating systems often cycle forever, which can be easily expressed with the **loop** statement. Both Ada and CHILL have a similar loop construct with conditional exits.

The **with** statement in Modula is similar to the same statement in Pascal, except that in Modula the **with** statement can enclose a list of statements, and it is always closed with **end**.

3.4 SUBPROGRAMS

Modula, just like Pascal, has the procedure and function as subprograms. Scope rules, and the association between formal parameters (mentioned in the heading of the procedure declaration) and actual parameters (mentioned in the call statement) are similar to Pascal. A function in Modula also has the keyword **procedure** in its heading. It can be distinguished from a proper procedure by the indication of the type of the result in the heading of the declaration.

In ISO Pascal conformant array parameters were introduced to make it possible to pass arrays of any size as actual parameters to a procedure. This is done differently in Modula. Instead of the following heading of the declaration of the procedure *countadult2* in Pascal (see section 2.4):

> **procedure** *countadult2* (**var** *p* : **array** *[lo..hi : integer]* **of** *person)* ;

we write in Modula:

> **procedure** *countadult2* (**var** *p* : **array** *integer* **of** *person)* ;

The bounds of the actual parameter can be obtained by the predefined functions *low* and *high* in Modula.

The procedure *countadult2* of section 2.4 could be programmed as follows (note that a **for** loop does not exist in Modula):

```
procedure countadult2 ( var p : array integer of person) ;
  var i : integer ;
begin
  i := low(p) ;
  loop
    with p[i] do
      if age < old then age := age + 1 end ;
      if age > 20 then counter := counter + 1 end
    end ;
    when i = high (p) exit ;
    i := i + 1
  end
end countadult2 ;
```

This procedure can be called with an array of *person* of any size.

In Modula the order of constant definitions, type definitions, variable declarations and (local) subprogram declarations within a subprogram is free (in Pascal the order was fixed, see section 2.4).

3.5 MODULES

A module is a collection of declarations of types, constants, variables and subprograms. It can also contain statements, e.g. to initialize the variables of the module. The declared objects are not visible outside the module, unless their names are exported by putting them in the **define**-list. Objects declared outside the module are not visible inside the module, unless their names are imported by putting them in the **use**-list. Hence a module allows precise control over the visibility of names. This considerably enhances the possibilities for reliable program design. It also provides a mechanism to define new data types together with the possible operations on objects of such types.

A schematic example of a module declaration is as follows:

```
module name ;
  define c, t1, v1, p1, p2 ;
  use e1, e2 ;
  const c = ... ;
  type t1 = ... ; t2 = ... ;
```

```
var v1 : t1 ; v2 : ... ; v3 : ... ;
procedure p1 (...) ... end p1 ;
procedure p2 (...) ... end p2 ;
procedure p3 (...) ... end p3 ;
begin
   statements
end name ;
```

The **define**-list can contain names of constants, types, variables and subprograms declared within the module.

When a subprogram is exported (*p1* and *p2* in the above example), it can be called from outside the module.

When a type is exported (*t1* in the example), variables of this type can be declared outside the module:

```
var x, y : t1 ;
```

Operations on variables of type *t1* have to be defined in the same module in which *t1* was defined. Types of this kind are called *abstract data types* In Modula exported operations are limited to procedures and functions operating on parameters of type *t1*. Even assignment statements and comparisons like:

```
x := y ;
if x = y then ...
```

are not allowed. If for example comparison between two variables of type *t1* is required, it can be defined within the module by an (exported) function accepting two parameters of type *t1* and delivering a boolean result.

When a variable is exported (*v1* in this example), its value can be read (provided its type has also been exported) but not modified outside the module. A new value can only be assigned through a call on a procedure declared within the same module, thus protecting the variable against unauthorized access.

Names not mentioned in the **define**-list are internal to the module, and cannot be referred to outside the module (*t2, v2, v3, p3* in this example).

This is checked by the compiler: no run-time checking is required.

The **use**-list contains the names of constants, types, variables and subprograms that are imported into this module and either exported from another module, or defined in the directly enclosing module.

The statements within the module (between **begin** and **end**) are executed when the module comes into scope, i.e. when the subprogram in which the module is declared, is called. This allows the initialization of variables inside the module, before any (exported) subprogram can be called. Note that the module itself cannot be called, but only its exported subprograms. Note also that the protection as provided by the module cannot be achieved by subprograms alone. If we were to change the module *name* in the example into a procedure, it would for example not be possible to call the procedures *p1* and *p2* directly.

The two major purposes of a module are:

- To group related subprograms which share internal variables, types, constants, and other subprograms. The module hides these internal objects and protects them from unauthorized use.

- To define abstract data types. The type is exported, together with the subprograms which specify the allowable operations on values of the type. The internal structure of the type is invisible outside the module.

A simple example of the first purpose is:

```
module members ;
   define countadult2, counter, members ;

   type members =
      record
         (* for definition see section 2.2.7 *)
      end ;
   var counter : integer ;

   procedure countadult2 ( var p : array integer of person) ;
      (* for body see section 3.4 *)
   end countadult2 ;
```

```
begin
  counter := 0
end members ;
```

The results of the calls on *countadult2* are accumulated in *counter*. The module *members* makes sure that:

- *counter* is initialized before *countadult2* can be called.

- it is impossible to change the value of *counter* outside the module (because export of variables is "read-only").

In the original solution (i.e. without the module) *counter* was declared as a global variable. This does not provide any protection against unauthorized modification.

An example of the second purpose (abstract data types) is:

```
module keymanager ;
  define key, getkey, available, assign, equal ;
  const nullkey = 0 ; lastkey = 99 ;
  type key = integer ;
  var presentkey : key ; available : boolean ;

  procedure getkey ( var k : key) ;
  begin
    if not available
      then k := nullkey
      else presentkey := presentkey + 1 ;
        k := presentkey ;
        available := presentkey < lastkey
    end
  end getkey ;

  procedure assign ( var x : key ; y : key) ;
  begin
    x := y
  end assign ;
```

```
procedure equal (x, y : key) : boolean ;
begin
  equal := x = y
end equal ;

begin
  presentkey := nullkey ;
  available := presentkey < lastkey
end keymanager ;
```

This module defines the type *key*, the procedures *getkey* (to get a unique key if there is one available) and *assign* and the function *equal*. Variables of type *key* can be declared and operated on, for example:

```
var frontdoor, backdoor : key ;

if available
  then getkey (frontdoor)
end ;
if not equal (backdoor, frontdoor)
  then assign (backdoor, frontdoor)
end ;
```

Outside the module the structure of *key* (i.e. that it is implemented as an integer between 0 and 99) is unknown. Hence a statement like:

```
frontdoor := 6
```

is illegal.

The module is a central concept in modern programming languages. In a slightly different form it is also present in Ada and CHILL.

3.6 PROCESSES

Concurrent actions in a program can be specified by *processes*. A process is a sequential (part of a) program and can be executed concurrently with other processes.

A process declaration is similar to a procedure declaration, with the keyword **procedure** replaced by **process**. As an example, consider the positioning of a robot-arm with a separate motor for each of the three dimensions:

```
type dimension = (xdim, ydim, zdim) ;

process move (dim : dimension) ;
var position : integer ;
begin
  loop
    readposition (dim, position) ;
    movetoposition (dim, position)
  end
end move ;
```

The process for one motor is specified as an infinite loop which

- reads a position from some table of positions

- moves the motor to that position

A process is started by a **process** statement, which looks like a procedure call:

```
move (xdim) ;
```

The **process** statement starts the process *move* as a separate action concurrently with all other already started (and not yet finished) processes. When control reaches the end of a process, this process ceases to exist (i.e. unlike the situation with a procedure-return, control is not returned to the process that started it). In many practical situations, however, processes are cyclic and never come to an end (as in the above example). It is possible to start the same process several times, with possibly different parameters, for example:

```
move (xdim) ; move (ydim) ; move (zdim) ;
```

Thus several *instances* of the same process are executing concurrently. In this case the movements of the three motors are controlled concurrently. Hence the final arm position may be reached more quickly than if the actions to move the motors were executed sequentially (this, however, depends upon the implementation).

Process declarations may not be nested, hence a process can only be declared at the outermost level (the main program). A **process** statement (to start a process) is only allowed in the main program.

The main program in Modula is written as an ordinary module. A schematic example of a Modula program with processes is:

> **module** *robot ;*
> *(* declarations, including process declarations, for example: *)*
> **process** *move . . . . .* **end** *move ;*
> . . . . . .
> **begin**
> *(* statements, including process statements, for example: *)*
> *move (xdim) ; move (ydim) ; move (zdim) ;*
> . . . . . .
> **end** *robot.*

Both Ada and CHILL have the concept of a process. CHILL is very similar to Modula in this respect, whereas Ada also provides facilities for nesting of process declarations.

3.7 COMMUNICATION BETWEEN PROCESSES

Processes usually are not independent of each other and therefore they have to cooperate in some way to achieve a common goal. This cooperation may take two forms:

- Communication, i.e. the sharing of data (and other resources) between processes. In Modula this is done through *interface modules.*

- Synchronization, i.e. one process waits until another process has reached a certain state. In Modula this is achieved by sending and waiting for *signals.*

An interface module is similar to a normal module. Shared variables between processes are declared local to an interface module and processes can access these variables through calling (exported) procedures declared local to the same interface module (called: *interface procedures*). The interface module (unlike a normal module) prohibits simultaneous access from several processes to the shared variables in order to keep the relation between these variables consistent. When a process is executing an interface procedure, another process calling the same or another procedure exported from the same interface module is delayed until the first process has completed its procedure (or starts waiting for a signal, see later on). Hence processes have mutually exclusive access to variables declared local to an interface module.

As a simple example consider two processes which produce a stream of characters and one process which consumes these characters. The communication between the producers and the consumer is done through an interface module which contains:

- An array *container* as a buffer for several characters to allow for temporary differences in speed between production and consumption.

- A procedure *put* to deposit a character in the buffer.

- A procedure *get* to retrieve a character from the buffer.

The *producer-* and *consumer* processes exchange characters via calls on the (exported) procedures *get* and *put*. A complete schema of a Modula program for this example is as follows:

```
module giveandtake ;

  process producer ;
  var ch : char ;
  begin
  loop
  .... put(ch) ....
  end
  end producer ;

  process consumer ;
  var ch : char ;
  begin
  loop
  .... get(ch) ....
  end
  end consumer ;
```

```
interface module exchange ;
  define put, get ;
  const max = 10 ; (* container size *)
  var container : array 1 : max of char ;
    in, out, n : integer ;

  procedure put (c : char) ;
  begin waitnonfull ;
    container[in] := c ;
    in := (in mod max) + 1 ; n := n + 1
  end put ;

  procedure get ( var c : char) ;
  begin waitnonempty ;
    c := container[out] ;
    out := (out mod max) + 1 ; n := n − 1
  end get ;

  begin (* statement part of exchange *)
    (* initialize variables *)
    in := 1 ; out := 1 ; n := 0
  end exchange ;

begin (* statement part of giveandtake *)
  (* start processes *)
  producer ; producer ; consumer
end giveandtake.
```

It is impossible to make any assumptions about the relative speed with which the processes proceed and the program should be correct in all possible situations. This induces the following requirements:

- a *producer* must be delayed when *container* is full and a *consumer* when *container* is empty.

- *put* and *get* must be executed in mutual exclusion.

The test whether *container* is nonfull or nonempty is executed in the beginning of the procedures. To facilitate these tests, the actual number of characters in *container* is recorded in the variable n. Later on these tests will be discussed in more detail.

The necessity for mutual exclusion in the execution of the procedures
get and *put* can be demonstrated as follows. Assume that a producer
has just filled the last slot and before updating *n* another producer calls
put. Without mutual exclusion this last producer could start executing
put, would conclude that *container* is not yet full and would deposit
his character, thus overwriting a character which has not yet been
retrieved.

The tests *waitnonfull* and *waitnonempty* could be implemented as follows:

```
(* waitnonfull: *)
loop
    when n < max exit
end ;

(* waitnonempty: *)
loop
    when n > 0 exit
end ;
```

However, this would imply that a *producer* calling *put* when $n = max$ is
looping continuously to test whether $n < max$ (thereby occupying the
processor). This is called *busy waiting*. During the continuously running
test of the condition $n < max$ the process *consumer* is not allowed to
enter the interface module and execute *get*. Hence no character would
be retrieved and a deadlock results because the condition $n = max$
would exist forever. Modula has the so-called *signals* to overcome this
problem.

A *signal* is a special predefined type, which cannot assume any value.
There are two predefined procedures and one predefined function which
can operate on signals (assume *s* is a variable of type signal):

- *wait(s)* : delay the process until another process sends *s*.

- *send(s)* : if there are one or more processes waiting for *s*, continue
  one of these processes. If there is no process waiting it has no
  effect.

- *awaited(s)* : true if there is at least one process waiting for *s*,
  otherwise false.

When a process executes *wait(s)* within an interface procedure, the mutual exclusion is released and a process waiting to enter the interface module is allowed to proceed.

When a process sends a signal *s* to another process within the same interface module, two possibilities arise: either the sending process or the receiving process continues (continuation of both processes is not allowed, because only one process can occupy the interface module). In Modula it is specified that the sending process is delayed and the receiving process is continued. The delayed process can be resumed when the other process either leaves the interface module or it starts waiting for some condition inside the interface module. Whether the delayed process actually continues immediately after one of these conditions becomes true depends upon the implementation of Modula and of the state of the other processes in the system.

The operations *waitnonfull* and *waitnonempty* in the interface module *exchange* can now be implemented with signals. The complete interface module can be expressed as follows:

```
interface module exchange ;
   define put, get ;
   const max = 10 ;
   var container : array 1 : max of char ;
      in, out, n : integer ;
      nonempty, nonfull : signal ;

   procedure put ( c : char) ;
   begin
      if n = max
        then wait (nonfull)
      end ;
      container[in] := c ;
      in := (in mod max) + 1 ; n := n + 1 ;
      send (nonempty)
   end put ;
```

```
procedure get ( var c : char) ;
begin
  if n = 0
    then wait (nonempty)
  end ;
  c := container[out] ;
  out := (out mod max) + 1 ; n := n − 1 ;
  send (nonfull)
end get ;

begin
  in := 1 ; out := 1 ; n := 0
end exchange ;
```

Note that during execution of the interface procedures the signals *nonempty* and *nonfull* may be sent many times without any effect because no process is waiting. This could be avoided by first testing whether there is a waiting process:

```
if awaited (s) then send (s) ;
```

As another example consider the positioning of the robot-arm from section 3.6. The processes repeatedly execute:

```
readposition (dim, position) ;
movetoposition (dim, position) ;
```

The robot-arm cycles through a number of fixed positions which are laid down in a table. Assume that the return from a call to *movetoposition* is carried out only after the completion of the mechanical movement. The three motors must be synchronized such that they can start their $(n+1)$th step only after the completion of step n for all three motors. This effect can be indirectly achieved by means of the procedure *readposition*, exported from the interface module *positionbuffer* as given below:

```
interface module positionbuffer ;
  define readposition ;
  use dimension ;
  const max = 30 ;
  var trajectory : array 1 : max, xdim : zdim of integer ;
    index, numberofwaiters : integer ;
```

```
    ready : signal ;

procedure readposition (ax : dimension ; var pos : integer) ;
begin
  if numberofwaiters < 2
    then
        numberofwaiters := numberofwaiters + 1 ;
        wait(ready) ;
        numberofwaiters := numberofwaiters − 1 ;
    else
        index := (index mod max) + 1 ;
        send(ready) ; send(ready)
    end ;
    pos := trajectory[index, ax]
  end ;

begin
    index := max ;
    numberofwaiters := 0 ;
    (* initialize trajectory *)
end positionbuffer ;
```

The variable *numberofwaiters* gives the number of processes waiting to
read a new position from the array *trajectory*. If *numberofwaiters* equals
two and the third process calls *readposition*, the index in the array is
incremented and the signal *ready* is sent to the waiting processes. These
(in turn) read their new position and leave the interface module. Finally
also the third process reads its new position and leaves *positionbuffer*.

3.8   DEVICE COMMUNICATION

A device can be thought of as a "hardware" process, which can communicate with other "regular" processes through an interface module.
As an example the process *consumer* in section 3.7 can be replaced
by a printer. When a regular process wants to print a character, it
sends this character to the interface module *exchange* by calling *put*.
The printer continuously calls on *get* to retrieve the next character
(if there is one) and prints it. However, in most practical situations
the printer is a passive device and cannot take the initiative to call
get. Instead the program has to execute some input/output instruction.

The printer usually sends an interrupt to the computer when it is ready
with the operation. Hence *get* should not be a (passive) procedure, but
an (active) process. Since regular processes may not be declared within
interface modules, Modula has a special type of interface module for
device communication, called a **device module**.

Within a **device module** there are procedures to communicate with
regular processes and device processes to communicate with devices. In
the device process, the statement **doio** represents the actual input/out-
put operation and serves as a "wait for interrupt". The device process
is suspended and the mutual exclusion on the device module is released
(compare with a regular process waiting on a signal within an interface
module). When the interrupt from the device occurs, the device process
can be continued at the statement following **doio**. Actual continuation
can only take place if the device module is not occupied by another
(device or regular) process.

When a device process sends a signal to another process executing an
(exported) procedure in the same device module, the device process
continues execution because it has a higher priority than a regular
process (note that this rule is an exception to the rule given in section 3.7). There are other special rules for device processes. Only a
single instance of a device process can be activated, they must not call
procedures imported into the device module and they must not send
signals to other device processes.

A device module contains machine-dependent information because the
input/output structure differs among the various computers. It must
also contain application dependent information, such as hardware priority, and addresses for devices and interrupt vectors.

The device module *printer* is an example of a device module in a PDP-
11† environment. In the heading of the device module the hardware
priority is specified.   All code within the device module is executed
at this priority. *Printerstatus* and *printerbuffer* are device registers for
serial output. Their addresses are specified in octal format (corresponding to PDP-11 conventions). Bit 6 of *printerstatus* controls inhibiting
and enabling of interrupts. In the heading of the device process the
interrupt vector address is specified to enable the system to return to

---

†PDP is a trademark of Digital Equipment Corporation

the statement following **doio** after the interrupt has occured.

The device module *printer* is as follows:

```
device module printer[4] ;
  define writech ;
  const max = 64 ;
  var printerbuffer [177566B] : char ;
      printerstatus [177564B] : bits ;
      in, out, n : integer ;
      nonfull, nonempty : signal ;
      container : array 1 : max of char ;

  procedure writech (ch : char) ;
  begin
    if n = max
      then wait (nonfull)
    end ;
    container[in] := ch ;
    in := (in mod max) + 1 ; n := n + 1 ;
    send (nonempty)
  end writech ;

  process driver[64B] ;
  begin
    loop
      if n = 0
        then wait (nonempty)
      end ;
      printerbuffer := container[out] ;
      out := (out mod max) + 1 ; n := n - 1 ;
      printerstatus[6] := true ;
      doio ;
      printerstatus[6] := false ;
      send (nonfull)
    end
  end driver ;
```

```
begin
    in := 1 ; out := 1 ; n := 0 ;
    driver
end printer ;
```

Note that implementation dependent information is completely confined to the device module. The code of the device module may be modified to drive e.g. a different printer, but as long as the procedure interface to the regular processes remains the same, it does not affect the rest of the program.

As another example consider a device module for the driving of the three motors controlling the position of a robot-arm (see sections 3.6 and 3.7). The process *move* calls the procedure:

$$movetoposition \ (dim, \ position) \ ;$$

and returns after the completion of the mechanical movement.

The procedure *movetoposition* first deposits the new position in the appropriate element of the array *coordinate* and sends the signal *start* to the device process for the appropriate direction. According to the rules, the device process which is waiting for *start*, now continues, performs the actual output to the device and starts waiting for an interrupt. The process *move* may now start waiting for the signal *ready[d]* in the procedure *movetoposition*. However it may also happen that this signal is sent by the driver process (to indicate the end of the mechanical movement) before the statement *wait(ready[d])* is executed. In that case the signal will be lost and, when eventually *wait(ready[d])* is executed, a deadlock results. Therefore the device process uses a boolean variable *reached* to indicate whether the mechanical movement has taken place. In *movetoposition* the process only waits for *ready[d]* if this variable is false i.e. if the mechanical movement is not completed.

A device module which includes a process for driving the x-direction motor is as follows:

```
device module motor[3] ;
    (* contains only driver process for x − position *)
    define movetoposition ;
    use dimension ;
    var coordinate : array xdim : zdim of integer ;
```

```
    start, ready : array xdim : zdim of signal ;
    reached : boolean ;
    xstatus [177234B] : bits ;
    xbuffer [177236B] : integer ;

  procedure movetoposition (d : dimension ; p : integer) ;
  begin
    coordinate[d] := p ;
    send (start[d]) ;
    if not reached
      then wait (ready[d]) ;
    end ;
  end movetoposition ;

  process xdriver[54B] ;
  begin
    loop
      wait (start[xdim]) ;
      xbuffer := coordinate[xdim] ;
      reached := false ;
      xstatus[6] := true ; doio ; xstatus[6] := false ;
      reached := true ;
      send (ready[xdim])
    end
  end xdriver ;

begin
  reached := false ;
  xdriver
end motor ;
```

Driver processes for the movement in y- and z-direction can be added in the same device module. Note that it is not allowed to start more than one instance of a device process.

Ada and CHILL have more primitive facilities for the programming of device communication.

3.9   DIFFERENCES BETWEEN MODULA AND MODULA-2

As was said in section 3.1, Wirth has designed a new language, called Modula-2. It inherited from Modula the name, the important module concept and a systematic modern syntax. From Pascal it inherited most of the remaining features. This section contains an overview of the main differences between Modula and Modula-2.

Cónstants are as in Modula, but constant expressions are allowed in constant definitions e.g

>   **const** *size = last − first + 1 ;*

Types in Modula-2 are closer to Pascal than to Modula. The same simple types are provided as in Pascal (including subranges). In addition the type *cardinal* (unsigned integers) and the type *bitset* (similar to *bits* in Modula) are predefined. The structured types are as in Pascal but the file type is absent. A procedure type is provided which denotes a procedure heading i.e. the procedure name and the formal parameter list, e.g.

>   **type** *action =* **procedure** *(var par : integer) ;*

Control statements are as in Modula. In addition a **for** statement is provided where optionally the increment of the control variable can be specified e.g.:

>   **for** *v := a* **to** *b* **by** *c* **do** ... **end** *;*

The module concept is more elaborate than in Modula. Exported objects can be denoted as *qualified*. This means that importing modules must reference the objects with a *qualified identifier* i.e. the name of the object must be prefixed with the (exporting) module name and a dot. In this way clashes between the same object names exported by different modules can be avoided. The following example clarifies this:

>   **module** *charbuf ;*
>   **export qualified** *get, put ;*
>
>   . . . .
>   **end** *charbuf ;*

```
module intbuf;
  export qualified get, put ;
  . . . .
end intbuf;

module client ;
  import charbuf.get, intbuf.get ;
  var ch : char ; i : integer ;
  . . . .
  charbuf.get (ch) ;
  intbuf.get (i) ;
  . . . .
end client ;
```

Import lists may be prefixed with an optional **from** followed by a module name e.g.:

from *intbuf* **import** *get* ;

This allows the use of *get* without qualifying it with *intbuf* (the effect is similar to that of a **with** statement when using record field names).

There is no distinction in Modula-2 between interface modules, device modules and ordinary modules. In fact interface modules and device modules can be implemented with the ordinary module together with the basic facilities as provided by the predefined module called *system*. This module exports a number of types and procedures which provide primitives needed for concurrency, input/output and "low-level" programming. Using these primitives, modules can be constructed with an abstract interface but a machine dependent implementation (like device modules in Modula).

The *system* module provides the facilities for concurrency on a conventional single processor system. These are of a rather primitive nature. They permit the declaration of quasi-concurrent processes which are similar to coroutines. The processes in Modula-2 cannot use the communication facilities as provided in Modula (interface module, signals). Instead only explicit transfer of the processor from the running process to another process can be programmed. For this purpose the procedure

procedure *transfer (* **var** *p1 , p2 :* **process** *) ;*

is provided. It suspends the calling process, assigns the processor to *p1* and resumes the process designated by *p2*.

In addition, the *system* module exports primitives for process creation (not for activation) and facilities for input/output (dependent on the target machine). For device drivers genuine concurrency can be achieved. With these primitive concurrency facilities and the module concept, higher level constructs can be programmed.

Modula-2 supports separate compilation. The module is used as a compilation unit. There are three kinds of compilation units:

- **main module**
  This constitutes the main program ; it does not export any objects.

- **definition module**
  This gives the definition of the exported objects: constants, types, variables, and procedure headings.

- **implementation module**
  This module implements the corresponding definition module i.e. the procedure bodies of the exported procedures, the definitions of exported types and variables, and possibly further declarations of internal objects.

As an example consider a definition module for the introduction of the concurrency facilities of Modula, written in Modula-2:

definition module *processscheduler ;*

    from *system* **import** *address ;*
    (this allows the use of "address" instead of "system. address" *)*

    export qualified
    signal, startprocess, send, wait, awaited ;

    type *signal ;*
    (The type definition is not given here. This is only allowed for pointer types and subranges of predefined types. *)*

procedure *startprocess (p: proc ; a: address ; n: cardinal) ;*
(start p with workspace a of length n *)*

procedure *send (var s: signal) ;*
(resumes first process waiting for s *)*

procedure *wait (var s: signal) ;*
(insert at end of queue waiting for s,*
*and resume any process that is ready *)*

procedure *awaited (s: signal): boolean ;*

end *processscheduler.*

This definition module can be separately submitted to the compiler and any modules importing the facilities that *processscheduler* exports can be compiled against this module. The implementation of this module (i.e. the bodies of the procedures and the definition of the type *signal*) is defined in an implementation module and can be developed (and compiled) separately. This stimulates top-down design with stepwise refinement.

Ada also separates the definition of a module (called *package* in Ada) from its implementation.

4 CHILL

4.1 INTRODUCTION

The use of computers for controlling switching systems has grown very
rapidly and presently all new systems are controlled by software. Some
properties of programs for telecommunication switching systems are:

- they are large and complex (program + data range from 500K
  bytes to many megabytes) ;

- they control real-time applications, i.e. time-constraints exist ;

- they must operate reliably, because PTT's require highly reliable
  telephone exchanges ;

- they must allow extensions and changes without disturbing the
  ongoing traffic.

These properties can serve also as a set of requirements for a language
to be used in switching systems. The CCITT (Comité Consultatif
International Télégraphique et Téléphonique) recognized in the early
70's the need for the use of a high level language because this would
make the users (i.e. the telephone administrations) more independent of
the manufacturers. In 1973 existing languages were evaluated against a
set of criteria but (not surprisingly at that time) none were considered
satisfactory. In 1975 a group was set up, chaired by Bourgonjon of
Philips' Telecommunicatie Industrie, to make a preliminary proposal
for a new language. This was presented in 1976. In the period until
1979 this proposal was evaluated and several trial implementations were
made which provided valuable feedback on the original design. The
language finally proposed, called CHILL (Ccitt HIgh Level Language),
was ready by the end of 1979. In November 1980 the CCITT's Plenary
Assembly approved it as an official CCITT Recommendation (Z.200
which has the status of a standard within the CCITT).

The original requirements for CHILL came from the switching system
area but they can be mapped on any large, reliable embedded computer
system. Hence CHILL is a "general purpose" language for embedded
computer systems and its facilities are comparable with those of Ada.

The type system of CHILL is much more elaborate than that of Pascal. Modules and processes in CHILL are similar to those in Modula but CHILL provides more facilities for communication and synchronization between (possibly distributed) processes. In addition, so-called exceptions can cause the execution of user-defined exception handlers in abnormal situations.

A CCITT Recommendation must be accepted unanimously by its members. In some situations this has led to syntax alternatives but, on the whole, the design did not suffer very much from the "committee effect".

Although CHILL has now been standardized by the CCITT work on several aspects of its use and implementation is continuing. The work within the CCITT is organized in study periods of four years. At the end of a study period there is a Plenary Assembly, which can approve new Recommendations. During the study period there can only be Draft Recommendations. For the current study period (1981-1984) the CCITT is paying special attention to:

- Programming support environments for CHILL.

- Extensions to the present definition in the areas of: input/output, timing, dynamic storage allocation, separate compilation and real arithmetic. Draft Recommendations to extend CHILL with dynamic memory allocation, input/output facilities and separate compilation have been agreed upon.

- Questions about compliance of compilers and programs to the CHILL definition.

- Training in the use of CHILL.

The official definition defines the language very precisely. It is therefore much more appreciated by compiler-writers than by "normal" CHILL users who find it difficult to read. This has hampered the spreading of information about CHILL. A Users Manual providing a definition of CHILL from the users' point of view is now available.

A number of manufacturers of telecommunication switching systems is now using CHILL for the programming of their new systems. Since the telecommunications community is strongly backing CHILL, its use in this area will grow rapidly. In other non-military areas there will be competition from Ada.

In the following sections a brief introduction to CHILL is given. Emphasis will be put on those parts which are different from Pascal and Modula, i.e. types, exceptions and the facilities for communication between processes.

4.2   TYPES

4.2.1   Introduction

As Pascal, CHILL also includes simple types, structured types and pointer types. In addition CHILL provides procedure types and several types related to concurrent processing. The latter types are not discussed here, but in section 4.7.

CHILL offers several facilities to control the representation of data in types (in Pascal there is only *packed*). These are discussed in section 4.2.12.

CHILL has two different ways to define types as is shown in section 4.2.13. This solves a problem with the typing system in Pascal and it provides a major improvement in the handling of types.

The terminology and keywords in CHILL often deviate from Pascal. A (not complete) list is given in Table 1. In the sequel the Pascal terminology is used as much as possible.

Before introducing the various types of CHILL, constant definitions and variable declarations will be discussed briefly.

4.2.2   Constant Definitions

Similar to Pascal (see 2.2.2) names can be introduced as synonyms for values of simple type, for example:

syn *first = 1, last = 9,*

old = 110, max = 100 ;

Pascal	CHILL
constant definition	synonym definition
const	**syn**
type	mode
type	**synmode** (or **newmode**,see 4.2.13)
enumeration type	set mode
(id1, id2,...,idn)	**set** (id1, id2,...,idn)
set type	powerset mode
set	**powerset**
record type	structure mode
record....end	**struct** (.....)
pointer type	reference mode
↑ (in type def.)	**ref**
↑ (dereferencing)	− >
variable	location
var	**dcl**

TABLE 1: corresponding terms in CHILL and Pascal

Pascal also allows constant definitions of string values. In CHILL this is extended to values of any type (e.g. also to array and record types). For example:

syn *yell = 'I like CHILL',*
   *initweek workweek = [(mon : wed) : false, (**else**) : true)] ;*

initweek is a value of the array type *workweek* (see 2.2.6). The elements indexed by *mon*, *tues* and *wed* are *false*, the other elements (indexed by *thur* and *fri*) are *true*. A structured constant can be assigned to a variable of the same type for example:

   firstweek := initweek ;

4.2.3   Variable Declarations

As in Pascal, all variables (called *locations* in CHILL) have to be declared
to be of a certain type. The declaration may specify an initialization of
the variable. This was not possible in Pascal. Some examples of variable declarations are:

> **dcl** *counter int :*= *first,*
>   *i index,*
>   *firstweek workweek :*= *initweek ;*

This declares *counter* of type *int, i* of type *index* and *firstweek* of type
workweek. It also initializes *counter* and *firstweek* to *first* and *initweek*
respectively.

Variables and types in CHILL can be given the attribute "read-only".
Assignments to read-only variables are prohibited, hence they must be
initialized in the declaration. For example:

> **dcl** *constfield* **read** *int :*= *10 ;*

Ada has the concept of constant variables. This more or less combines
the facilities provided by constant definitions and "read only" variables
in CHILL .

4.2.4   Simple Types

CHILL has three predefined types: *int* (integer), *bool* (boolean) and *char*
(character). A CHILL implementation may specify other predefined
integer types, e.g. longint, shortint.

As in Pascal, user-defined simple types can be defined by enumerating
all the values of the type (see 2.2.3), for example:

> **synmode** *day* = **set** *(mon, tues, wed, thur, fri, sat, sun) ;*

Like Pascal (see 2.2.4) CHILL allows the definition of subranges of
simple types, called *range type.* For example:

> **synmode** *workday* = *day (mon : fri),*
>   *index* = *int (first : last),*

years = *int (0 : old) ;*

Extension of CHILL with a *real* type is being considered by the CCITT.

4.2.5   Structured Types

Like Pascal, CHILL has, as structured types, the array, the record (called *structure* in CHILL) and the set (called *powerset* in CHILL). In addition it has a separate string type which can be used for character- as well as for bit-strings. CHILL makes a distinction between static types, where all information about the type is known at compile-time, and dynamic types, where certain information about the type is determined at run-time, i.e. the index bounds of arrays, the size of strings and the variant part of a variant record. In certain contexts values of dynamic type have to be handled through pointers, e.g. in case of formal array parameters. Sections 4.2.6 to 4.2.9 introduce the structured types.

There is no file type because CHILL does not currently include facilities for input-output. However, a draft recommendation for extending CHILL with file types and operations on files exists. This is expected to become an official recommendation at the CCITT Plenary Assembly in 1984.

4.2.6   Array Types

Arrays in CHILL are almost equivalent to arrays in Pascal. Some examples of array type definitions are (compare with 2.2.6):

synmode *workweek* = **array** *(workday) bool,*
    letterfreq = **array** *('A' : 'Z') int ;*

As in Pascal, the index can be any discrete type and arrays can have any number of dimensions. The declaration of an array may specify an upper bound which is smaller than the original upper bound in the type definition, for example:

dcl *letters letterfreq ('P') ;*

As shown already in section 4.2.2, CHILL allows the specification of array-values called array tuples. Some examples of different specifications for the same array tuple of type *workweek* are:

[false, false, false, true, true]
[(mon : wed) : false, (thur : fri) : true]
*[(thur : fri) : true, (***else***) : false]*

When all elements have the same value, the following form can be used:

[(*) : false]

It is possible to specify part of an array-variable by listing the lower and upper bounds (which of course must not exceed the bounds specified in the type definition or variable declaration). For example:

dcl *firstweek workweek ;*
firstweek (mon : wed) := [(*) : false] ;
if *firstweek (mon : tues)* = *firstweek (thur : fri)* **then** ....

Such a part of an array-variable is called a *subarray* if the bounds can be determined statically (i.e. at compile-time) and an *array slice* if the bounds can only be determined at run-time. The predefined function *upper*, which delivers the highest index of the specified array, can be used when handling dynamic arrays. The lower bound of dynamic arrays is fixed by the type definition.

4.2.7 String Types

Strings in CHILL can either be character strings or bit strings. The character string type is similar to the *packed array of char* in Pascal; the length is fixed by the type definition and single characters can be accessed using an integer index. In the type definition the length of the string is given, for example (compare with 2.2.6):

synmode *words* = *char (last) ;*
dcl *command words, c char ;*
command := '*off hook* ' *;*
c := command (2) ;

The string type *words* is 9 characters long, indexed from *0* to *last*-1 (in Pascal: *1* to *last*).

Just like arrays in CHILL, strings can be declared with an upper bound smaller than the original one as given in the type definition.

As in Pascal, strings can be compared. In addition it is possible to form a part of a string by specifying an index range. Similar to arrays, this is called either a *substring* (bounds are static) or a *string slice* (bounds are dynamic). Concatenation of strings is also allowed, for example:

```
dcl long_ command char (12) ;
command (0 : 2) := ' on' ;
long_ command := 'not'//command ;
```

The first assignment statement replaces 'off' by ' on' in *command*. The second assignment statement concatenates the string 'not' with *command*, thus resulting in the string 'not on hook ' being assigned to *long_ command*.

Operations on bit strings are the same as for character strings (including the forming of substrings and concatenation). In addition logical operators can be applied (**and, or, xor, not**). For example (compare with Modula, 3.2):

```
synmode bits = bit (16) ;
dcl status, mask bits ;
mask := H'3D00' ;
status := mask and H'9F0' ;
```

Bit string literals can be specified in binary, octal or hexadecimal notation. Similar to arrays, the predefined function *upper* delivers the upper index of the specified bit or character string.

4.2.8   Record Types

Records are called *structures* in CHILL. An example of a record type definition in CHILL (c.f. section 2.2.7):

```
synmode person =
  struct (
    name words,
    age years,
    present workweek,
    citizen bool
  ) ;
```

Accessing fields in a record is done as in Pascal, for example:

```
dcl johnson, harris person ;
johnson.age := 43 ;
harris.present (tues) := true ;
```

In CHILL, records can have one or more variant parts which may be defined anywhere in a record. In Pascal there is only one variant part which has to follow the fixed part. Both languages allow a variant part to contain a record with again a variant part. An example of a variant record type definition is (see 2.2.7) :

```
synmode new_person =
  struct (
    name words,
    age years,
    present workweek,
    citizen bool,
  case citizen of
    (true) : pensionno int,
    (false) : status set (permanent, temporary, visiting),
      passportno int
  esac
  ) ;
```

Within a variant part, the last alternative may also be specified with **else**. As an example, the variant part of *new_person* could also be written as follows:

```
synmode new_person =
  struct (

    . . .

  case citizen of
    (true) : pensionno int,
```

```
else status set (permanent, temporary, visiting),
    passportno int
esac
) ;
```

A variant record can be declared either with or without parameters specifying the particular variant. For example in:

```
dcl ferguson new_ person,
    smith new_ person (true) ;
```

the variable *smith* is declared to have the variant-alternative belonging to the tagfield (i.e. the field *citizen*) value *true*. It would be illegal trying to change the variant by assigning *false* to the field *citizen*. However for *ferguson* no parameter is specified and *ferguson*'s tagfield may be changed. For example the following assignments are legal:

```
ferguson.citizen := false ;
ferguson.status := visiting ;
ferguson.citizen := true ;
ferguson.pensionno := 35173 ;
smith.pensionno := 23619 ;
```

However

```
smith.citizen := false ;
```

is illegal.

Just as it provides array tuples, CHILL also provides record tuples, i.e. values of a certain record type, for example:

```
ferguson := ['Ferguson ', 45, [(*) : false], true, 35173] ;
```

It is also possible to explicitly specify the fields, for example:

```
ferguson :=
    [ .name : 'Ferguson ',
    .age : 45,
    .present : [(*) : false],
    .citizen : true,
    .pensionno : 35173 ] ;
```

The field names must be specified in the same order in which they appear in the record definition.

4.2.9 Set Types

In CHILL, the equivalent of the Pascal **set** is called **powerset**, for example (c.f. section 2.2.8):

> **synmode** *wdayset* = **powerset** *workday* ;
> **dcl** *week1, week2 wdayset* ;

Set-values are written as in Pascal. Also the operations on set-values are the same but the operators **or** and **and** are used instead of + and * to indicate union and intersection. In addition, CHILL provides the operation **xor** (those members which are only in one of the operands) and **not** (those members which are not in the operand). For example (see 2.2.8, comments in CHILL are enclosed by /* and */) :

> *week1* := *week1* **xor** *week2* ; /* *week1 contains mon, wed, fri* */
> *week2* := **not** *week1* ; /* *week2 contains wed, thur* */

4.2.10 Pointer Types

Pointers in CHILL are called *references*. There are three kinds of pointers:

- *bound references* : the type definition includes the (static) type of the variables where the pointer may refer to (also c.f. Pascal section 2.2.10).

- *free references* : may refer to variables of any (static) type.

- *rows* : pointers to objects of dynamic type (string and arrays with statically unknown bounds or records with statically unknown variant).

Pascal pointers can only point to dynamically created variables (via the procedure *new*, see 2.2.10). CHILL pointers can also point to "normally" declared variables. At present, however, the dynamic creation of objects in CHILL is restricted to variables on the stack (via

a call on a predefined procedure *getstack*), i.e. the objects disappear
automatically when leaving the directly enclosing block. An extension of CHILL for the Pascal-like dynamic creation of variables has
been agreed upon. Formal standardization of this extension awaits the
CCITT Plenary Assembly in 1984.

An example of a bound-reference type (c.f. section 2.2.10):

synmode *ref_to_person* = **ref** *person* ;
dcl *harris person*,
    p, q ref_to_person ;

p := − >*harris* ;

Now *p* points to the record variable *harris*. Its fields can be accessed
directly, or indirectly via dereferencing of *p*:

p − >.*citizen* := *true* ;

A complete record assignment is also possible:

p − > := ['*Harris*   ', *23*, [(*) : *true*], *true*] ;

As in Pascal, pointers can be assigned to each other, for example:

q := *p* ;

Only pointers of type **row** can refer to variables whose size is unknown
at compile time. For example, assuming:

synmode *line* = *char(80)* ;
dcl *line_ref* **row** *line*,
    current_line line,
    i, j int (0 : upper (current_line)) ;

then *line_ref* can point to a string slice (i.e. statically unknown bounds):

line_ref := − >*current_line (i : j)* ;

4.2.11   Procedure Types

A procedure type definition allows the dynamic manipulation of procedures (i.e. the code of the procedure), e.g. a procedure definition can be assigned to a variable of a procedure type or it can be a parameter of a procedure. Procedure types do not exist in Pascal, Modula or Ada. Modula-2 does include procedure types.

A procedure type definition specifies its name, the type of the parameters and the result (if any), and the formal exceptions (if any, see section 4.8). An example of a procedure type definition is:

> **synmode** *similar* $=$ **proc** *(words)* **returns** *(bool)* ;

The most important application of procedure types is probably their use as types of formal parameters of a procedure. In this way procedures can be passed as parameters to other procedures. This, however, can also be done in Pascal without procedure types. Procedure types, in addition, allow the declaration of procedure variables, and hence the dynamic manipulation of procedure definitions. Consider for example the following two procedure definitions:

> *is_ off :*
> **proc** *(w words)* **returns** *(bool)* ;
>   **return** *w* $=$ *'off hook '* ;
> **end** *is_ off ;*
>
> *is_ on :*
> **proc** *(w words)* **returns** *(bool)* ;
>   **return** *w* $=$ *' on hook '* ;
> **end** *is_ on ;*

Both procedure definitions are of the same type as the procedure type *similar*: they have one value parameter of type *words* ($=$ *char(last)*, see 4.2.7), and a result of type *bool*. Hence it is possible to assign *is_ on* and *is_ off* to a (procedure) variable of type *similar*. For example, assuming the declarations

> **dcl** *state similar,*
>   *command words,*
>   *b bool ;*

the following assignments could be done:

state := is_ off ; b := state (command) ;
state := is_ on ; b := state (command) ;

First the procedure definition *is_ off* is assigned to the procedure variable *state*. The next statement executes *state* with *command* as actual parameter (i.e. *is_ off* is executed) and assigns the result to *b*. The last two statements show how another execution of *state* can result in the execution of a different procedure (*is_ on* in this case).

4.2.12 Representation Specification

CHILL offers several facilities to specify the way data are represented and to control the storage allocation for enumeration, array and record types. Just like Pascal the values of an enumeration type are ordered, the first is mapped on 0, the second on 1, etc. (see 2.2.3). CHILL allows this implicit numbering scheme to be overwritten by explicitly specifying the internal representation. This can for example be useful when enumeration types are used for input/output where they have to be mapped on external hardware, for example:

synmode *switch* = **set** *(off = 0, half = H'40, full = H'80) ;*

For structures and arrays it is possible to specify **pack** to indicate a more efficient packing of data. For example:

synmode *byte* = *int (0 : 255) ;*
dcl *x* **array** *(1 : 100) byte* **pack** *;*

For a 16-bit computer this would probably result in two array elements per computer word.

The internal representation of arrays and records can be even more precisely controlled by specifying bit-positions. An example for records is:

dcl *calldata*
   struct *(*
     junction_ no int **pos** *(0),*
     answer_ time int (0 : 100) **pos** *(1, 0 : 6),*

standard__rate bool **pos** *(1, 7)*
) ;

The **pos** attribute specifies the relative position:

- *junction__ no* in word 0

- *answer__ time* in word 1 bits 0 - 6

- *standard__ rate* in word 1 bit 7.

4.2.13   New Types and Type Compatibility

Pascal's major contribution was the concept of *type*. However the original definition contained many ambiguities in the rules about type compatibility. As a simple example consider the following type definitions (in CHILL notation):

synmode *t1* = **array** *(1 : 10) int,*
  t2 = **array** *(0 : 9) int,*
  t3 = **array** *(0 : 9) int,*
  t4 = *t3 ;*

In the original Pascal definition it was not quite clear whether the above defined types are different or the same. This is important in order to establish rules about type compatibility for assignment and parameter passing. ISO Pascal is much more precise in this respect but it restricts the possibilities.

CHILL (and also Ada) makes a distinction between two possible effects of a new type definition:

- The new type remains compatible with the type it is derived from according to certain rules which have to be defined.

- The new type is completely different from the type it is derived from.

Both possibilities can be specified in CHILL, the first by the already used **synmode** definition, the second by a so-called **newmode** definition. For the above example the type *t1* is the same as the type **array** *(1:10)int*, and *t2* is the same as **array**(0:9)int. According to the CHILL rules on type compatibility (which differ considerably from those of ISO Pascal and those of Ada) it can be concluded that the types *t1* and *t2* are the same because:

- They have the same element type (*int*).

- The "parent-type" of the indexes are the same (both subranges of *int*).

- The number of elements is the same (= 10).

- Their representation is the same (in fact the representation specification is absent for both, see 4.2.12).

Hence a variable of type *t1* can be assigned to a variable of type *t2*. Similarly an actual parameter of type *t1* can be used when a formal parameter of type *t2* is specified.

A simple example of a **newmode** definition together with a variable declaration is:

```
newmode clear_ day = day ;
dcl c clear_ day,
    d day ;
```

Now *clear_ day* and *day* are completely different types (although th y share the literals defined for type *day*, i.e. *mon, tues*, etc). Hence the following statement is illegal:

```
c := d ;
```

Explicit type conversions are possible. Some legal assignments are:

```
c := mon ;
c := clear_ day (d) ; /* type conversion */
```

Ada also has two mechanisms for the definition of new types, but the rules for type compatibility are rather different (see 5.2.12).

4.3   STATEMENTS

All statements which can enclose other statements (e.g. loop and
conditional statements) have as closing symbol the reverse spelling of
the starting keyword (c.f. Modula, where it was always **end**):

> **if** . . . **fi**
> **case** . . . **esac**
> **do** . . . **od**

The conditional statements are the **if**- and the **case** statement. The **if**
statement is the same as in Modula (with the **elsif** clause). The **case**
statement has, compared to Pascal and Modula, some extra possibilities:

- It includes an **else** clause which is executed if none of the cases
  match;

- A single case can be specified by a subrange of a discrete type
  (in Pascal all cases have to be enumerated explicitly);

- One case can be specified by several conditions (a decision table).

An example of the first two extensions is:

> **case** *command (i)* **of**
>   *('+', '−') : sign := true ;*
>   *('0' : '9') : digit := true ;*
> **else** *no_ digit := true ;*
> **esac** *;*

Note that in Pascal the subrange *'0' : '9'* would have to be enumerated
explicitly and the **else** part is not allowed.

An example of a **case** statement with a decision table is:

> **case** *i, command (i)* **of**
>   *(0), ('+', '−') : sign := true ;*
>   *(else),('0' : '9') : digit := true ;*
> **else** *no_ digit := true ;*
> **esac** *;*

This specifies that:

- if $i = 0$ and $command(i) =$ '$+$' or '$-$' then $sign := true$

- if $i \mathrel{/}= 0$ and '0' $<= command(i) <=$ '9' then $digit := true$

- in all other cases, $no\_\,digit := true$.

CHILL has one general loop statement (**do..od**) with the possibility to specify:

- Repetition in a **for** clause,

- Conditional execution in a **while** clause (this may also be put after an already present **for** clause),

- A **with** clause,

- An **exit** statement to leave the loop.

An example of a **for** clause with **exit** statements is (c.f. Modula section 3.3):

```
lab:
do for i := 0 to upper (command) ;
  if command (i)=' # '
    then cross := true ;
      exit lab ;
  elsif command (i)=' $ '
    then dollar := true ;
      exit lab ;
  fi ;
od ;
```

Note that in the **exit** statement the label of the loop to be exited is specified. This allows the termination of more than one (nested) loop. The loop variable i is implicitly declared. This is different from Pascal and Modula but the same as in Ada.

Some special forms of the **for** clause allow:

- specification of the step size,

- stepping automatically through:

    – all values of a discrete type,

    – all values of an expression of type powerset,

    – all array-elements.

For example:

```
do for element in firstweek ;
   element := false ;
od ;
```

assigns *false* to all elements of the array *firstweek*. Note that *element* is implicitly declared for the **do** statement.

An infinite loop can be made by:

```
do for ever ; . . . . od ;
```

An example of a **while** clause is (c.f. section 2.3):

```
current := head ;
do while current /= null ;
   . . . .
   current := current − >.next ;
od ;
```

An example of a **with** clause is (c.f. section 2.3):

```
do with harris ;
   name := 'Harris    ' ;
   age := 23 ;
   present := [(*) : true)] ;
   citizen := true ;
od ;
```

Note that the above **do with** statement can be written also as a single tuple assignment (see e.g. the assignment of a tuple to *ferguson* in 4.2.8).

There is a **goto** statement which cannot branch outside of a procedure.

With an **assert** statement a condition can be tested. If the test fails, an exception occurs (see section 4.8). For example:

assert $i <=$ *upper (command)* **and** $i >= 0$;

tests whether i is a valid index for the string *command*.

CHILL has a so-called **begin..end** block which is like the compound statement in Pascal (see section 2.3) but it is extended with the possibility to specify local declarations and definitions. Ada has a similar facility.

Other statements in CHILL deal with the calling of procedures, the starting of processes, the communication between processes and the causing of exceptions. These statements are not discussed here, but in the sections 4.4 (procedures), 4.6 (processes), 4.7 (communication between processes) and 4.8 (exceptions).

4.4 SUBPROGRAMS

Subprograms in CHILL are, as usual, the procedure and the function. In both cases the same keyword **proc** is used in the heading of the declaration (similar to Modula).

Like Pascal and Modula, parameters can be passed *by value* or *by reference* (called *by location* in CHILL and indicated by the keyword **loc**). An example of a function definition with value parameters (c.f. Pascal section 2.4):

```
older:
proc (p1, p2 person) returns (bool) ;
    return (p1.age > p2.age) ;
end older ;
```

CHILL allows the specification of three "flavours" of formal value parameters with the attributes **in**, **out** and **inout**. In common with Pascal and Modula the formal parameters behave as local variables of the subprogram. The differences are:

- **in** specifies that the initial value of this local variable is taken
  from the actual parameter (as in Pascal). The actual parameter
  can be either a value or a variable. The **in** attribute is assumed
  by default, as in the procedure *older*.

- **out** specifies that the (final) value of this local variable is assigned
  to the actual parameter when leaving the procedure. The actual
  parameter must be a variable.

- **inout** specifies a combination of **in** and **out**. The actual parameter
  must be a variable.

Ada provides similar facilities for formal value parameters but does not
include parameter passing by reference.

Array and string parameters with statically unknown bounds have to
be handled via **row**s in CHILL, i.e. via a pointer to the array. The
procedure *count_ adult2* in section 3.4 would look as follows when coded
in CHILL:

```
newmode people = array (1 : max) person ;

count_ adult2 :
proc (p row people) ;
   do for each in p — > ;
      do with each ;
         if age < old
            then age := age + 1 ;
         fi ;
         if age > 20
            then counter := counter + 1 ;
         fi ;
      od ;
   od ;
end count_ adult2 ;
```

Note that *each* is implicitly declared within the **do for** statement. Note
also that *p* is an **in** parameter because no results are returned to the
variable *p*, although results are returned to the array to which *p* refers.

This procedure can be called with any row-value pointing to an array of *person* provided its index-range does not exceed the range *1* to *max*.

Functions cannot only return a value but also a variable (called *location* in CHILL). Thus a function call can be placed at the left-hand side of an assignment statement. As an example consider a function which returns the element of a *person* with a specified name (assuming that there is at least one person with that name):

```
somebody :
proc (p row people, ident words) returns (person loc ) ;
  do for elem in p — > ;
    if ident = elem.name
      then return elem ;
    fi ;
  od ;
end somebody ;
```

Assuming the declarations:

```
dcl programmers people (30) ;
  ref_ programmers row people := — >programmers ;
```

then the following statement assigns *true* to the field *citizen* of the person with the name *mrs chill*:

```
somebody (ref_ programmers, 'mrs chill').citizen := true ;
```

Pascal, Modula and Ada do not provide this facility.

In CHILL (like Ada) definitions and declarations may be in any order (in Pascal the order is fixed, see 2.4).

4.5   MODULES

CHILL includes (similar to Modula) the module concept (see section 3.5). CHILL uses the keywords **grant** and **seize** to export and import names (in Modula: **define, use**; in Modula-2: **export, import**).

There are small differences between CHILL and Modula regarding the purpose of the module. These differences are explained using the module *key_ manager* as defined in section 3.5, which in CHILL looks as follows:

```
key_ manager:
module
  grant key, get_ key, available ;
  syn null_ key = 0, last_ key = 99 ;
  newmode key = int (null_ key : last_ key) ;
  dcl present_ key key := null_ key,
      available bool := present_ key < last_ key ;

  get_ key:
  proc (k key out ) ;
    if not available
      then k := null_ key ;
      else present_ key := succ (present_ key) ;
        k := present_ key ;
        available := present_ key < last_ key ;
    fi ;
  end get_ key ;

end key_ manager ;
```

In CHILL the primary purpose of the module is the precise control over the visibility (and consequently useability) of names. The special rules of Modula regarding the exporting of type names and variable names do not exist in CHILL. However CHILL allows a more precise control over what can be done with names using the **newmode** definition, the **forbid** clause in exported record types, and the **grant pervasive** facility. Thus abstract data types can be defined, although some inherited operations (assignment and test for (in)equality) cannot be suppressed.

In the module *key_ manager* the exported type *key* is defined with a **newmode** definition. This ensures that, outside the module, no type can be defined which is compatible with the type *key*. Hence any operations possible on values of type *key* must be defined within the module and exported from the module. In practice this is the same as in Modula, but in CHILL it is achieved via the newmode concept, and in Modula via additional rules on the module concept. There is one situation in which this leads to a clear difference. The literals of a type are also the literals of the type defined via a newmode definition. Hence all integers are literals for the newmode *key*. For example:

house :
module
  seize *key ;*
  dcl *frontdoor key,*
    gate int ;

  . . . .
  frontdoor:= gate ; /* illegal in CHILL and Modula */
  frontdoor := 6 ; /* legal in CHILL, illegal in Modula */
  end *house ;*

The procedures *assign* and *equal* (see original definition of *keymanager* in 3.5) are not needed in CHILL because assignment and comparison for (in)equality are always defined for values of an exported newmode.

In CHILL it is only allowed to grant names which have their defining occurrence within the module (or a nested module). In Modula this was not defined which left many open questions because the same object can then be reached via different names.

When a record type or an enumeration type is exported, there are concealed names within the type, which are not explicitly mentioned in the **grant** statement, i.e. the field names in a record type and the names denoting the values of the enumeration type. Consider for example the following module:

telephone :
module
  grant *subscriber_ type, subscriber_ data ;*
  newmode
    subscriber_ type = set *(analog, digital),*
    subscriber_ data =
      struct *(*
        telephone_ number int,
        no_ of_ sets int,
        ana_ dig subscriber_ type
) ;
  . . . .
  end *telephone ;*

The concealed names in the enumeration type are *analog* and *digital*. In the exported record type the concealed names are the fieldnames *telephone_ number, no_ of_ sets* and *ana_ dig*. In CHILL there are

precise rules about the implications of concealed names when the type
to which they belong is imported (Modula was not precise in this
respect). It is possible for example to refer directly to a field name
of an imported record type:

```
user :
module
  seize subscriber_ data ;
  dcl my_ data subscriber_ data ;
  my_ data.no_ of_ sets := 2 ;
    . . . .
end user ;
```

However the visibility of fieldnames can be controlled by the exporting
module through the specification of **forbid** followed by the fieldname(s)
in the **grant** statement. All fieldnames can be made invisible by specifying **forbid all**. For example:

```
grant subscriber_ data forbid all ;
```

makes all fieldnames invisible outside the module *telephone*.

Names denoting the values of an enumeration type are called *weakly
visible* in the importing module. There are special rules governing the
name binding of weakly visible names.

It is possible to grant a name **pervasive**, for example:

```
grant subscriber_ data forbid all pervasive ;
```

This makes *subscriber_ data* automatically visible in all modules which
could have seized it. This is useful for modules containing subprograms
which are considered as "libraries".

CHILL has some shorthand notations for granting and seizing. When
all names defined in a module are granted, the construct

```
grant all ;
```

can be used. Similar facilities exist for seizing:

```
seize all ;
```

seizes all names which are (strongly) visible immediately outside the module, while for example:

seize *telephone* **all** *;*

seizes all names that are granted by the module *telephone* and are (strongly) visible immediately outside the seizing module.

In Ada the **package** provides similar facilities as the **module**. The mechanisms to make names visible to other packages are different from those of CHILL, but for many practical situations the results are similar. For example in Ada it is also possible to control the visibility of field-names of exported record types.

4.6 PROCESSES

In CHILL processes can be declared in a way similar to a procedure declaration with the keyword **proc** replaced by **process**. The example of a process declaration for the robot arm as introduced in section 3.6 is in CHILL as follows:

```
newmode dimension = set (xdim, ydim, zdim) ;
move :
process (dim dimension) ;
  dcl position int ;
  do for ever ;
    read_ position (dim, position) ;
    move_ to_ position (dim, position) ;
  od ;
end move ;
```

Processes can only be declared at the outermost level. A process can be started from another process or from the *imaginary outermost process* (see later).

A process can be started many times with, possibly different, parameters. Every start of a process creates a new instance of the process declaration. This instance can be identified by a unique instance value which belongs to a special predefined type called *instance*. The instance value is used for communication between process instances through **signals** (see 4.7.4). For other ways of communication between processes (**regions** and **buffers**) the instance value of a process is not used.

The starting of instances of the process *move* is done in CHILL with a **start** statement as follows:

  start *move (xdim) ;*
  start *move (ydim) ;*
  start *move (zdim) ;*

If the instance values are required, variables of type *instance* have to be declared and a slightly different form of the **start** statement is used:

  dcl *xinst, yinst, zinst instance ;*
  start *move (xdim)* **set** *xinst ;*
  start *move (ydim)* **set** *yinst ;*
  start *move (zdim)* **set** *zinst ;*

After the execution of the **start** statement, the instance variable mentioned after **set** contains the unique instance value of the started process instance.

The process concept in CHILL is very similar to that of Modula:

- Processes can only be declared at the outermost level;

- Process declarations look like procedure declarations;

- An instance of a process can be started by an explicit **start** statement in which parameters can be specified.

The main differences are:

- CHILL allows the starting of a process from any other process including the *imaginary outermost process*. In Modula only the latter is possible.

- In CHILL a process instance can be identified with a unique instance value. In Modula a process instance is anonymous.

- In CHILL a process instance can terminate itself by executing a **stop** statement.

In Ada a process is handled as a type, and an instance of a process is considered as a variable declaration of the type. Process definitions can be nested.

A program in CHILL is a collection of modules. This is surrounded by the *imaginary outermost process* which is started by the underlying operating system.

4.7 COMMUNICATION BETWEEN PROCESSES

4.7.1 Introduction

CHILL provides three mechanisms for communication and synchronization between processes:

- **regions**. These are comparable with interface modules in Modula. They provide mutual exclusive access to shared variables declared within a region.

- **buffers**. They are a kind of mailbox, in which values of a certain type can be deposited and retrieved by different processes.

- **signals**. They contain a list of values of specified types and can directly be transmitted from one process to another without any intermediate buffering at CHILL level.

There are several reasons why CHILL provides three different mechanisms for process communication:

- The ideas about what is the best method of communication between processes have not yet been stabilized in the world of programming language design. It would be too early to supply only one method of communication.

- Experience with communication between processes in a distributed system (without common memory between processors) is very limited. One communication mechanism may not be able to function optimally in both distributed and common memory architectures.

The three communication mechanisms can be used together in one program but, in practice, one or, at most, two mechanisms will be chosen. For a common memory architecture regions and/or buffers will probably be the natural choice. For a distributed architecture signals are more suitable because they do not need data shared between processes.

4.7.2   Regions

A region is similar to a CHILL module with mutually exclusive access to the procedures exported from the region. Variables shared between processes are declared local to a region. Synchronization between processes is achieved by **delay** and **continue** statements operating on a variable of type **event**. The CHILL region is very similar to the interface module in Modula. The **event** type in CHILL compares to the **signal** type in Modula. The CHILL statements **delay** and **continue** map on the predefined procedures *wait* and *send* in Modula.

The following example implements in CHILL the character buffer as defined in Modula (section 3.7, interface module *exchange*). Note the absence of a statement part for initialization in the region. All initializations are done as part of the declarations of local variables.

```
exchange :
region
  grant put, get ;
  syn max = 10 ;
  dcl container array (1 : max) char,
    in, out int := 1,
    n int := 0,
    nonfull, nonempty event ;

  put :
  proc (c char in ) ;
    if n = max
      then delay (nonfull) ;
    fi ;
    container (in) := c ;
    in := (in mod max) + 1 ; n := n + 1 ;
```

```
      continue (nonempty) ;
   end put ;

   get :
   proc (c char out ) ;
      if n = 0
         then delay (nonempty) ;
      fi ;
      c := container (out) ;
      out := (out mod max) + 1 ; n := n − 1 ;
      continue (nonfull) ;
   end get ;

 end exchange ;
```

Regions can - just like processes - only be defined at the outermost level of the program.

4.7.3 Buffers

Buffers are a kind of mailbox with slots through which processes can deposit and retrieve messages of a certain type.

In the declaration of a buffer, the type of the slot has to be made explicit. Also a length (i.e. the number of slots) may be given, in which case a process is delayed when it tries to deposit a value in a full buffer and it is continued when a slot becomes available.

If the buffer is declared within a process only the process itself can operate on this buffer. Buffers declared at the outermost level of the program can be used for communication between processes. Several processes can send/receive values to/from the same buffer variable.

The example of section 4.7.2, i.e. the region *exchange* can be replaced by a simple buffer declaration. An equivalent CHILL program for the complete module *giveandtake* (Modula, section 3.7) of which the module *exchange* was only a part, is as follows:

```
syn max = 10 ;
dcl container buffer (max) char ;

producer :
process ( ) ;
  dcl ch char ;
  do for ever ;
    . . send container (ch) ; . .
  od ;
end producer ;

consumer :
process ( ) ;
  dcl ch char ;
  do for ever ;
    receive case
      (container in ch) : /* statements */
    esac ;
    /* statements */
  od ;
end consumer ;

start consumer ; start consumer ; start producer ;
```

The **receive buffer** statement has some additional possibilities as shown in the next example (assume *error* has been declared as some buffer variable):

```
dcl send_ process instance ;
receive case set send_ process ;
  (container in ch) : /* statements */
  (error in e) : /* statements */
else /* statements */
esac ;
```

When, upon entering the **receive buffer** statement, there is a value either in *container* or in *error*, this value is received, the instance value of the sending process is assigned to *send_ process* and the appropriate statements are executed. When both buffers contain values, only one value is received (which one is unknown). The instance value of the process whose value is received is assigned to *send_ process*. When both buffers are empty, the statements in the **else**-part are executed, and the value of *send_process* is undefined.

4.7.4 Signals

Signals can be sent directly from one process instance to another one. Any intermediate buffering is taken care of by the underlying system. The **send** and **receive** statements for signals are similar to the corresponding statements for buffers. A signal definition, however, is completely different from a buffer definition.

A signal definition can be considered as the creation of a message channel between two or more processes. A signal is not a "type" in CHILL, hence there are no variable declarations for signals.

The example of the module *giveandtake* (section 3.7), which was programmed with buffers in section 4.7.3, would look very similar when signals were used, except for the actual signal definition:

signal *channel* = *(char)* **to** *consumer ;*

which replaces the buffer declaration. Otherwise the text remains the same, provided there is only one instance of the process *consumer* (which is actually the case). If there is more than one instance, the **send** statement must mention to which instance the signal has to be sent. For example, assuming *inst* is of the type *instance* and contains the correct instance value:

send *channel (ch)* **to** *inst ;*

The **receive signal** statement has the same possibilities as the **receive buffer** statement as mentioned at the end of section 4.7.3.

Because signals are sent directly from one process instance to another, they are particularly suitable for use in distributed systems.

The use of signals is now demonstrated with the example of the robot which was introduced in section 3.6 and elaborated in 3.7. The process *move* will be slightly different because communication has to take place via signals and not via procedure calls as in Modula. The (passive) interface module *positionbuffer* in Modula is replaced by an (active)

process called *set_position*. It is assumed that the actual motor rotation is controlled by a driver process, of which there are three instances.
The code for this process is outside the scope of this example.

The complete program is as follows:

```
newmode dimension = set (xdim, ydim, zdim),
   instdriver= array (dimension) instance ;
   /* instance value array for driver process */
signal coordinate = (int) to move,
   move_ arm = (int) to driver,
   ready to set_ position,
   reached to move ; /* sent from driver process */

move :
process (dim dimension) ;
   do for ever ;
     send ready ;
     receive case
       (coordinate in position) :
          send move_ arm (position) to instdriver (dim) ;
     esac ;
     receive case
       (reached) : ; /* wait until motor positioned */
     esac ;
   od ;
end move ;

set_ position :
process ;
   syn max = 10 ;
   dcl instmove array (dimension) instance,
     trajectory array (1 : max, dimension) int,
     index int (1 : max) := 1,
     no_ of_ waiters int (0 : 3) ;
   do for d in dimension ;
     start move (d) set instmove (d) ;
   od ;
   do for ever ;
     no_ of_ waiters := 0 ;
     do while no_ of_ waiters < 3 ;
```

```
      receive case
         (ready) : no_ of_ waiters := no_ of_ waiters + 1 ;
         esac ;
      od ;
      do for d in dimension ;
         send coordinate (trajectory (index, d)) to instmove (d) ;
      od ;
      index := (index mod max) + 1 ;
   od ;
end set_ position ;

start set_ position ;
```

The signal *coordinate* is defined as a signal to the process *move*. This means that it can only be sent to an instance of *move*. The **to**-part is optional. If omitted, the signal can be sent to any process. The signal *coordinate* is sent by the process *set_ position* and it transmits the value of the next coordinate to an instance of *move*.

The signal *move_ arm* replaces the call of the procedure *move_ to_ position* in the Modula example. It is sent by an instance of *move* and it transmits the next coordinate to an instance of the driver process. When the motor has actually reached its position, the driver process sends the signal *reached* to the instance of *move*.

The signal *ready* is used for the synchronization between the three motors and it is send by all instances of *move* to the process *set_ position*.

The process *set_ position*, after initializing *index*, starts three instances of *move*. Then it waits for the signals *ready* which are sent by the three instances of *move*. After receipt of these signals it transmits the new position to the instances of *move* and updates *index*.

4.8   EXCEPTIONS

CHILL allows the handling of exceptions, i.e. exceptional conditions occurring during the execution of a program. This is not possible in FORTRAN and Pascal or even in Modula. However, for embedded computer systems, where the execution of the program is directly influencing, and is influenced by some external physical process, the program should be able to handle all run-time error conditions. A well-known example is *overflow*. When it occurs, the program may not stop, but some sensible action, e.g. reporting the error and trying to recover from it, should be done. Ada also allows the handling of exceptions.

CHILL has nine language defined exceptions. Some examples are:

- *overflow*, occurring in arithmetic operations for example.

- *rangefail*, caused by value out of range and indexing or sub-stringing outside index boundaries for example.

- *empty*, caused by dereferencing an empty reference (i.e.= *null*) for example.

- *tagfail*, caused by accessing fields of a variant record with illegal tagfields for example.

In addition to the nine CHILL-defined exceptions, there are two other exception categories:

- Any CHILL implementation may specify additional predefined exceptions.

- The user can generate his own program-defined exceptions by means of the **cause** statement.

When an exception occurs, the appropriate (see later) exception handler is executed. An exception handler is enclosed by the symbols **on** and **end**. In between it looks like a **case** statement: the exception names are mentioned, followed by a statement list (which may be empty). There is also an optional **else** part followed by a statement list which is entered if none of the exception names match. An example of an exception handler is:

```
on
   (overflow) : /* statements */ ;
   (rangefail) : /* statements */ ;
else : /* statements */ ;
end ;
```

An exception handler can be appended to:

- A statement (including initialization in a declaration). After execution of the handler control is given to the next statement.

- A procedure definition. After execution of the handler control is given to the statement following the procedure call (unless otherwise directed in the exception handler).

- A process definition. After execution of the handler, the process is terminated.

When handling exceptions occurring inside a procedure, it may be desirable to handle them at the point where the procedure was called rather than inside the procedure definition. For this purpose a list of formal exceptions can be given in the procedure heading which means that whenever these exceptions are caused inside the procedure, they are considered to be caused where the procedure was called. This is also called: exception propagation. For example:

```
traffic_ handling :
proc ( ) exceptions ( congestion, timeout) ;
  if /* some condition */
    then cause abort ;
  fi ;
  if /* some other condition */
    then cause congestion ;
    else cause timeout ;
  fi ;
end on
  (abort) : /* some action */ ;
end traffic_ handling ;
```

In the above example all exceptions are user-defined. The exceptions *congestion* and *timeout* will be passed to the calling point, while *abort* is handled within the procedure.

At the calling point *congestion* and *timeout* could be handled immediately by appending a handler to the procedure call statement:

```
traffic_ handling( )
  on
    (congestion) : /* statements */ ;
    (timeout) : /* statements */ ;
  end ;
```

or the exceptions can be handled by appending the handler to the
enclosing procedure (if it exists), or the enclosing procedure heading
can mention their names again as formal exceptions, and so on.

The appropriate handler for an exception E occuring at a statement S
can be determined statically as follows:

- It is appended to S,

- or it is appended to a compound statement directly enclosing S,

- or it is appended to the procedure directly enclosing S,

- or the directly enclosing procedure has E in its formal exception
  list,

- or it is appended to the process directly enclosing S.

This also holds when an exception occurs when evaluating a declaration.
There is a special rule when an exception occurs inside an exception
handler.

When no exception handler can be found according to the above strategy, the program is in error.

Ada has a different strategy for locating the appropriate exception
handler. Formal exceptions do not exist, and the search always continues along the dynamic calling chain.

4.9   PIECEWISE COMPILATION

The current definition of CHILL does not mention the possibility to
compile a part of a program. Current implementations often use the
module as the part that can be handled separately. A Draft Recommendation on what is called *piecewise compilation* is ready.   This
Recommendation adds the following new facilities to CHILL:

- A *spec module* which defines the properties of all the names
  exported by the piece(s) it belongs to. This allows independent compilation of pieces. Unlike Ada, these names and there

properties do not represent the defining occurrences of the names.

- A flexible system for name qualification, to reduce name clashes when many pieces are put together.

- A mechanism to refer to the text of a piece which is kept somewhere else.

- Better facilities for the handling of names exported by modules which are meant to be libraries.

The piecewise compilation proposals[†] allow the independent development and compilation of pieces, but when the program is put together the interfaces between the pieces are checked.

In Ada separate compilation is defined in the language. Packages, (comparable with the module in CHILL), procedures, and processes can be separately compiled.

---

† Bishop, Bordelon, Cheung, Feay, Louis, Smedema
Separate compilation and the development of large programs in CHILL.
Proceedings IEE 5th International Conference on Software Engineering for
Telecommunication Switching Systems, Lund, Sweden, July 1983

5   ADA

5.1   INTRODUCTION

In the early seventies, the United States Department of Defense (DoD) perceived that it needed to take action to control the rapidly rising software costs. The fact that within DoD over 300 programming languages were used for the production of software for operational systems - so called embedded systems - was thought to be a major cause of the cost explosion. Therefore, a project was started aimed at a drastic decrease in the number of languages used by either selecting a suitable existing language or creating a new language.

The first step toward this goal was to develop requirements for such a language. Participants in this development were DoD on one side and the computing community at large on the other side. Several refinements were made to the original set of requirements, reflecting criticism of those who responded. The documents were entitled: Strawman, Woodenman, Tinman, Ironman and finally Steelman requirements.

The evaluation of existing programming languages resulted in the following major conclusions:

- No language was suitable as it was;

- A single language was a desirable, if not essential, goal;

- The state-of-the-art allowed the design of such a language;

- Development should not start from scratch but should be done on the basis of a suitable language.

After the publication of the Ironman document, proposals for the design of a language, based upon either Pascal, PL/1 or ALGOL 68, were invited. From the seventeen received proposals, four were selected as basis for the actual design of the language. In order to allow unbiased comparison of the designs, they were given the names Blue, Red, Green and Yellow respectively. All four designs were based on Pascal. As a result of an evaluation by widely respected experts, the designs Blue and Yellow were discarded. The final selection was done in 1979 and Green was considered the better choice for a variety of reasons.

This language was the product of a design team headed by Ichbiah, then working for CII-Honeywell/Bull in France. One of the reasons Green was selected was the stability of the design, as opposed to the dramatic changes that were made to the Red design as a result of the public evaluation. Ironically, Ada - as the language was baptized, after the Countess of Lovelace, who is said to have been the first programmer as assistent to Charles Babbage - has changed considerably since her birth!

The language has been standardized by ANSI early in 1983. International standardization is sought but there are some formal problems related to DoD's position on the control of the definition of Ada and its compilers.

A large effort is directed towards the definition of a so-called Ada Programming Support Environment (APSE). An approach, similar to the one adopted for the language requirements has led to a set of requirements, known as the Stoneman document.

In the following sections a brief introduction to Ada is given. Emphasis will be put on those parts which are different from Pascal and Modula, i.e. the typing system, exceptions, the facilities for communication between concurrent processes, generics and separate compilation.

5.2   TYPES

5.2.1   Introduction

Like Pascal, Ada contains simple types and structured types. Pointer types do exist in Ada, but are of a different character from those known in Pascal. In addition Ada provides types related to concurrent processing. The latter types will not be discussed here, but in section 5.6.

Ada offers several facilities to control the representation of data in types (in Pascal there is only *packed*). These will be discussed in section 5.2.11.

Ada, more or less like CHILL, has two ways of defining types; a newly introduced type is either a new type definition or it is derived from an already existing type. New types are incompatible with all other types, derived types can be converted to the parent type.

Before introducing the various types of Ada, variable declarations and constant definitions are discussed briefly.

5.2.2   Variable declarations

All variables have to be declared to be of a certain type. The declaration may specify an initialization of the variable. This is not possible in Pascal. Some examples of variable declarations are:

> *counter : integer := 1 ;*
> *i : index ;*

This declares *counter* to be of the (predefined) type *integer* and *i* of type *index*. It also initializes *counter* to *1*. Note that there is no keyword for variable declarations in Ada (c.f. **var** in Pascal and Modula, **dcl** in CHILL).

5.2.3   Constant definitions

In Ada, constant definitions as such do not exist. However, a variable can be declared with the attribute **constant** and given a value. Assignments to such variables are prohibited (c.f. the **read** attribute in CHILL, section 4.2.3). The constant definitions of section 2.2.2 can be programmed in Ada as follows:

> *first :* **constant** *:= 1 ;*
> *last :* **constant** *:= 9 ;*
> *old :* **constant** *:= 110 ;*
> *max :* **constant** *:= 100 ;*

Pascal also allows constant definitions of string values. In Ada this is extended to values of any type (e.g. to array- and record types), for example:

```
yell : constant string := "I like Ada" ;
initweek : constant workweek :=
    ( mon..wed => false, others => true ) ;
deferred : constant some_private_type ;
```

Note the omission of the value for the constant variable *deferred*. This is allowed only for so-called private types; the value must be given in the *private* part of a package. (see 5.2.10 and 5.5.3).

These constants can now be used to initialize variables, for example:

```
firstweek : workweek := initweek ;
```

5.2.4   Simple types

There is a number of predefined types in Ada. They fall in the categories: *boolean, integer* (a number of types providing different ranges of values depending on the implementation), *float* (a number of types, as for integer), *character, duration* (implementation dependent). Also, types with range constraints are predefined for *natural* (the positive integers) and *priority* (an implementation defined range of integer values). As in Pascal, user defined simple types can be defined by enumerating all the values of the type (see 2.2.3), for example:

```
type day is ( mon, tues, wed, thur, fri, sat, sun ) ;
```

Like Pascal, Ada allows the definition of subranges of simple types (see 2.2.4) in a subtype declaration, for example:

```
subtype workday is day range mon..fri ;
subtype index is integer range first..last ;
```

Ada, unlike CHILL, offers several possible ways to declare variables of a non-integer numeric type. The two categories are floating point types, in which case the required number of significant digits must be specified, and fixed point types, where the required absolute precision must be given.

Examples:

    — — *comment in Ada begins with* ”— — ” *and ends*
    — — *at the end of the line*
    type *my— real* **is digits** *8 ;*
    type *another— real* **is digits** *10* **range** *1.0 .. 2.0 ;*
    — — *these were floating point types*
    type *fixed* **is delta** *0.0125 ;*
    type *money* **is delta** *0.01* **range** *0.0 .. 1000.0 ;*
    — — *and these were fixed point types*

5.2.5   Structured types

Like Pascal, Ada has the array and the record as structured types.
Ada does not provide set types but these can be implemented relatively
easily with boolean arrays (see section 5.3). In addition it has a separate
string type which can be used for character strings.

Input/output is defined in Ada through standard packages. Files are
handled in those packages by *limited private* types (see section 5.5.3).
Hence, no language defined file type exists, as in Pascal.

5.2.6   Array types

Arrays in Ada are almost equivalent to arrays in Pascal. Some examples
of array type definitions are:

    type *workweek* **is array** *(workday)* **of** *boolean ;*
    type *letterfreq* **is array** *(character* **range** *'A' .. 'Z')* **of** *integer ;*

As in Pascal, the index may be of any discrete type and arrays can have
any number of dimensions. Ada allows the specification of array values,
called array aggregates. Some examples of different specifications for
the same array aggregate for the array type *workweek* are:

    (false, false, false, true, true) ;
    (mon..wed => *false, thur..fri =*> *true) ;*

(thur..fri => true, **others** *=> false) ;*
(false,false,false, **others** *=> true) ;*

Array type definitions may leave the actual index bounds undefined.
An example of a so-called unconstrained array type:

type *matrix* **is array** *(integer* **range** *<>, integer* **range** *<>)* **of** *real ;*

The actual index bounds must then be given in the variable declaration:

rotation : matrix (1..20, 1..20) ;

It is possible to specify a consecutive part of a one dimensional array
variable (called a *slice*) by giving the lower and upper bounds of the
index (which of course must be within the bounds specified).   For
example:

firstweek : workweek ;
firstweek (mon..wed) := **(others** *=> false) ;*
if *firstweek (mon..tues) = firstweek (thur..fri)* **then** ...

Associated with arrays are attributes which serve to make available the
bounds of the index type as well as the number of elements of the array
for each dimension.   For example *workweek'first, workweek'last* and
workweek'length give the lower bound, the upper bound and the number
of elements of an array of type *workweek* respectively. Attributes may
be applied to both the types and the variables of that type, hence
firstweek'last is also valid.

5.2.7   String types

Strings in Ada are one-dimensional arrays of characters, indexed by
values of the predefined type *natural.* The length of the string is not
given in the type definition, but must be given in the declaration of a
string, for example:

command : string (first..last) ;
c : character ;
command := *"off hook " ;*
c := command (2) ;

Alternatively, one could define a subtype:

```
subtype words is string (first..last) ;
  command : words ;
```

Strings can be compared. In addition, it is possible to form a substring by specifying an index range. Concatenation of strings is possible, for example:

```
long_ command : string (1..12) ;
command (1..3) := " on" ;
long_ command := "not" & command ;
```

which results in "not on hook" being assigned to long_ command.

5.2.8   Record types

An example of a record definition in Ada (c.f. Pascal, section 2.2.7):

```
type person is
  record
    name : words ;
    age : years ;
    present : workweek ;
    citizen : boolean ;
  end record ;
```

Accessing fields in a record is done in a way similar to Pascal, for example:

```
johnson, harris : person ;
johnson.age := 43 ;
harris.present (tues) := true ;
```

In Ada, record types may contain *discriminants*. Such a discriminant may be used to specify a bound of an index of a component array or used as a parameter of a variant part. An example of a discriminant (*size*) which specifies an index bound of an array is:

```
type bucket (size : integer range 0 .. 100) is
  record
     pos : integer range 0..100 := 0 ;
     value : string (1..size) ;
  end record ;
```

An example of a discriminant used to specify a variant alternative (c.f. tagfield in Pascal, section 2.2.7) is:

```
type visa is (permanent, temporary, visiting) ;
type newperson (citizen : boolean) is
  record
     name : words ;
     age : years ;
     present : workweek ;
     case citizen is
       when true =>
          pensionno : integer ;
       when false =>
          status : visa ;
          passportno : integer ;
     end case ;
  end record ;
```

Like in Pascal, there is only one variant part which has to follow the fixed part. Within a variant part, the last alternative may also be specified with **others**, for example:

```
type newperson (citizen : boolean) is
  record
     name : words ;
     age : years ;
     present : workweek ;
     case citizen is
       when true =>
          pensionno : integer ;
       when others =>
          status : visa ;
          passportno : integer ;
     end case ;
  end record ;
```

A variant record can be declared either with or without parameters
specifying the variant. However if the variant is not specified then the
type definition must include a default value for the discriminant (see
below). For example in:

> *smith : newperson (true) ;*
> *ferguson : newperson (false) ;*

the variable *smith* is declared to have the variant-alternative *true* and
it would be illegal trying to change the variant by assigning *false* to
the discriminant. Similarly, *ferguson* is declared to have the variant-
alternative belonging to the discriminant value *false*. Some examples
of legal assignments are:

> *ferguson.passportno := 156845 ;*
> *ferguson.status := visiting ;*
> *smith.pensionno := 23619 ;*

However

> *smith.citizen := false ;*

is illegal.

Just like array aggregates, Ada also provides record aggregates, i.e.
values of a certain record type, for example:

> *ferguson :=*
>   *(false, "Ferguson ", 45, (**others** => false), permanent, 235677) ;*

It is also possible to explicitly specify the fields, for example:

> *ferguson :=*
>   *(citizen => false ,*
>   *name => "Ferguson " ,*
>   *present => (**others** => false) ,*
>   *age => 45 ,*
>   *passportno => 235677 ,*
>   *status => permanent) ;*

The field names do not have to be specified in the same order in which
they appear in the record definition.

In a record type definition initial values may be specified for (some of) its fields. Such initial values are assigned to the fields when a variable of that type is declared. Discriminants can be given default values which may be overruled in a variable declaration of the type. Subtypes of a record type may be defined in which a discriminant is given a fixed value. For example assume:

```
type device is (printer, drum, disk) ;
type peripheral (unit : device := disk) is
   record
      . . .
   end record ;
```

which defines a record *peripheral* with a discriminant *unit* of type *device* and the default value *disk*. A subtype definition may overrule this default, for example:

```
subtype drum_unit is peripheral (drum) ;
```

Some examples of variable declarations are:

```
line_printer : peripheral (unit => printer) ;
-- overruled default value
disk_unit : peripheral ; -- default value
```

The omission of a discriminant value in a variable declaration is only permitted if the type definition specifies a default value. Hence the variable declaration

```
ferguson : newperson ;
```

is illegal. The variant of variables for which no discriminant value is specified in the declaration (*disk_unit* for example) can be changed by assigning a complete record aggregate.

5.2.9 Access types

Variables of access type are pointers to other variables.

```
type ref_to_person is access person ;
type connection is access newperson ;
p1,p2 : ref_to_person ;
```

q : connection ;

The accessed objects are dynamically created by an allocator (similar to the procedure *new* in Pascal, see 2.2.10). This allocator indicates the type of the accessed object. The allocator may contain initializing values for the created objects and, if applicable, must contain the value for the discriminant, for example:

p1 := **new** *person ;*
q := **new** *newperson (citizen* => *true) ;*

Whenever a selected component is specified, dereferencing is automatic (see 2.2.10).

q.age := *38 ; — — dereferencing*
p2 := *p1 ; — — no dereferencing*
*p2.*all := *p1.*all *; — — dereferencing;* **all** *denotes the entire record*

The created objects remain allocated as long as they are accessible, i.e. as long as they can be designated by some name. Note that no explicit release of allocated variables is possible (in Pascal there is a procedure *dispose* for that purpose, see section 2.2.10).

5.2.10   Private types

In support of abstract data types, Ada provides type definitions the details of which can only be used inside the package where the type is defined. Outside that package, such details are inaccessible. Such types are called private types in Ada. For further details see section 5.5.3.

5.2.11   Representation specification

Ada offers several facilities to specify the way data are represented and to control the storage allocation for enumeration, array and record types. The values of an enumeration type are ordered. Ada allows the overruling of the numbering scheme used by the compiler for the representation of the enumeration values by explicitly specifying the internal representation. The integer values specified must satisfy the ordering relation of the enumeration type as defined in the language. This may be useful when enumeration types are used for input/output, where they have to be mapped on external hardware, for example:

```
type switch is (off, half, full) ;
for switch use
  (off => 0, half => 16#40#, full => 16#80#) ;
  —— the notation 16#...# indicates number base 16
```

For records and arrays it is possible to specify *pack* to indicate that storage efficiency should be the main concern when selecting an internal representation. This is done through a **pragma** which is a directive to the compiler, for example:

```
type byte range is 0..255 ;
type byte_array is array (1..100) of byte ;
pragma pack (byte_array) ;
```

The internal representation of records can be even more precisely controlled by specifying bit-positions, for example:

```
word : constant := 2 ; —— wordsize in addressing units
type call_data is
  record
    junction_no : integer ;
    answer_time : integer range 0..100 ;
    standard_rate : boolean ;
  end record ;
for call_data use
  record at mod 2 ;
    junction_no at 0 * word range 0..15 ;
    answer_time at 1 * word range 0..6 ;
    standard_rate at 1 * word range 7..7 ;
  end record ;
```

The representation clause specifies that each *call_data* variable has to be aligned at an even address and furthermore specifies the relative positions of the components within the record, giving both relative address and bit position.

For variables, as well as for subprograms, tasks etc. an address may be specified, e.g. to associate machine code with a subprogram name. For example:

control : switch ;
for *control* **use at** *16#4000# ;*

5.2.12   Derived types and type compatibility

Type equivalence is defined in terms of name equivalence. Thus two types which have been given different names are different, even if they have the same structure. However, subtypes of the same basetype are compatible with each other. For example in:

type *rainy_ day* **is** *day ;*

the type *rainy_ day* is a distinct type, not compatible with *day*.

Ada allows the definition of *derived types* from already defined types. Such types are not compatible with the parent type from which they were derived (as for "normal" types). However, all operations applicable to the parent type are inherited by the derived type. This applies also to subprograms with formal parameters of the parent type. Moreover, explicit conversion from a type to its parent type and vice versa is possible. As an example consider the following derived type declaration:

type *clear_ day* **is new** *day ;*

The type clear_day inherits the literals and all operations that are defined for *day*, but it is a distinct type. Explicit conversion of the one type to the other is possible. Assuming the variable declarations:

c : clear_ day ;
d : day ;

some examples of legal and illegal assignments are:

c := mon ; — — legal
c := d ; — — illegal
c := clear_ day (d) ; — — legal through type conversion

Type compatibility rules in CHILL and Ada are very different (see section 4.2.13). The "normal" type definition in CHILL (*synmode*) is closest to the *derived type* in Ada, while the *newmode* concept in CHILL is somewhat similar to a "normal" type in Ada. However, there are many differences.

5.2.13   Overloading

Ada allows the use of the same name for different entities, provided it is possible to determine which entity is meant when such a name is used. The multiple use of names in this manner is called overloading. As an example the overloading of enumeration literals will be given:

type *day* **is** *(mon, tues, wed, thur, fri, sat, sun)* ;
type *body* **is** *(sun, earth, moon)* ;

The literal *sun* has been overloaded. It may, clearly, only be used where its type can be determined from the context. If a reference is needed to *sun* in places where such is not possible, one of the qualified expressions *day'(sun)* or *body'(sun)* must be used.

Overloading also applies to names of subprograms and operators; more details will be given in section 5.4.

CHILL does not allow overloading.

5.3   EXPRESSIONS AND STATEMENTS

Expressions are built from variables, constants and all the well-known operators. The operators $=$ and $/=$ (equality and inequality) are defined for any type except limited private type (see section 5.5.3) and task type (see section 5.6), provided that both operands are of the same type. Additional to the logical operators **and** and **or**, there exist operators **and then** and **or else** which are called short circuit control forms (not available in Pascal, Modula and CHILL). The consequence of the use of these operators is that the right operand is not evaluated if the value of the left operand already determines the value of the result. So, it is legal to write (see 2.2.1 for declarations):

if *d1* **in** *workday* **and then** *firstweek (d1)*
  then ....

whereas in

if *d1* **in** *workday* **and** *firstweek (d1)*
  then ....

the right operand is illegal when the left operand has the value false,
i.e. when *d1* is either *sat* or *sun*.

Ada allows the operators **and** and **or** to be applied to entire arrays
of type boolean. The result is again an array of type boolean where
the elements are the results of the application of the operator to the
corresponding elements of the operand arrays. This feature can be used
to implement sets, for which no type is provided in Ada.

Ada has an operator for concatenation (&) applicable to one-dimensional
arrays of any type and an operator for exponentiation (**).

Ada (like CHILL) allows statements to be grouped into so-called block
statements. In such a block it is possible to declare objects locally, like
variables and tasks. For example:

declare
  i, j : integer ;
begin
  — — *statements*
end *;*

Like Modula and CHILL (but unlike Pascal) Ada has closing symbols for all control statements. Those closing symbols make all the
begin..end pairs for compound statements needed in Pascal superfluous.
Ada has different closing symbols for the various control statements:
end if, **end case** and **end loop**.

Just as Modula and CHILL, Ada allows the contracted form **elsif** which
saves an **end if**.

Compared with Pascal, Ada's **case** statement has two extensions:

- It includes an **others** clause which is executed when none of the other cases match;

- A single case can be specified by a subrange of a discrete type.

Ada does not provide decision tables as CHILL does (see section 4.3).

The example of section 4.3, written in Ada:

```
case command (i) is
  when '+'|'-' => sign := true ;
  when '0'..'9' => digit := true ;
  when others => no_ digit := true ;
end case ;
```

As in Pascal, Modula and CHILL, it is required in Ada that all cases are covered, i.e. there is exactly one branch for every possible value of the controlling expression. Any violation of this rule can be detected statically, i.e. at compile time.

The dummy statement in Ada is explicitly represented by the **null** symbol. It is not, as in ALGOL 60 or Pascal, represented by the empty sequence of symbols.

Ada has three forms of **loop** statement. As in Pascal, there is the traditional iteration with a **for** clause:

```
for i in firstweek'range
  loop
    firstweek (i) := false ;
  end loop ;
```

sets all elements of *firstweek* to false using the array attribute *range*. *Range* is defined as the subtype that extends from the lower bound of the (first) index of the array to the upper bound of the (first) index of the array. As opposed to Pascal, but like CHILL, the control variable *i* is implicitly declared.

The second form is a **loop** statement preceded by a **while** clause, also known from Pascal (see section 2.3):

```
  current := head ;
while current /= null
  loop — — process all elements of a chain
    . . . .
    current := current.next ;
  end loop ;
```

Ada does not provide a **repeat until** statement. There is a more general **loop** statement where the termination condition may occur at any place within the loop. To leave the loop, the **exit** statement is used, for example:

```
loop
  i := i + 1 ;
exit when sentence (i) /= ' $ ' ;
end loop ;
```

is the equivalent of the Pascal repeat statement mentioned in section 2.3 and

```
for i in command'range
  loop
    if command (i) = ' # '
      then cross := true ;
        exit ;
    elsif command (i) = ' $ '
      then dollar := true ;
        exit ;
    end if ;
  end loop ;
```

is the equivalent of the CHILL loop statement mentioned in section 4.3.

An **exit** statement may only appear within a loop but may cause termination of more than one (nested) loop, which is achieved by labelling the loop and using the appropriate label name in the **exit** statement.

A **goto** statement is available in Ada. This transfers control to a labelled statement, subject to some restrictions concerning nested statements. There is no label declaration as in Pascal.

A **with** statement as provided in Pascal and CHILL to allow unqualified access to field names in a record is not provided in Ada. The **with**-clause in Ada has quite a different purpose and will be discussed in section 5.9.

5.4 SUBPROGRAMS

As in Pascal, subprograms are procedures and functions (see section 2.4).

Subprograms may have formal parameters each of which must be declared in the subprogram heading. The type of each formal parameter must be defined, as in Pascal. Note that this implies that formal parameters can, for example, be tasks (see section 5.6) but not subprograms, since a subprogram type does not exist in Ada.

For the association between formal and actual parameters each formal parameter has one of three possible modes (attributes):

- **in**:
  The formal parameter is a local constant whose value is provided upon entry of the subprogram by the corresponding actual parameter. This is similar to *call by value* in Pascal. For functions, **in** is the only possible mode.

- **out**:
  The formal parameter is a local variable whose value is assigned to the corresponding actual parameter upon exit from the procedure. The actual parameter must be a variable.

- **in out**:
  This is a combination of the **in** and **out** modes. The value of the actual parameter is copied to the local variable when entering the procedure and the then current value of the local variable is copied to the actual parameter when leaving the procedure. This description should not be taken as a basis for programming because, in the case of aliasing, special care must be taken. The actual parameter must again be a variable.

If no mode is given then it is **in** by default.

Note that, inside the subprogram, modification of a selector, e.g. a global variable that is used to index an array in an actual parameter, does not affect that actual parameter.

Arrays as formal parameters may have unspecified bounds (see section 3.4 for a description of the problem). Ada calls this an unconstrained array type and uses $<>$ (the so-called box symbol) to indicate the range of such an array (see section 5.2.6).

The procedure that counts the number of adults in an array of *person* (see section 3.4) could be programmed as follows:

```
type list_ of_ person is array (integer range <>) of person ;
procedure count_ adult2 (p : in out list_ of_ person) is
begin
  for i in p'range
    loop
      if p (i). age < old
        then p (i). age := p (i). age + 1 ;
      end if ;
      if p (i). age > 20
        then counter := counter + 1 ;
      end if ;
    end loop ;
end countadult2 ;
```

An example of a function is (compare with sections 2.4 and 4.4):

```
function older (p1, p2 : person) return boolean is
begin
  return (p1. age > p2. age) ;
end older ;
```

A function can be designated not only by an identifier such as *older* but also by a character string denoting an operator such as $>$. A function so designated provides an additional overloading of the language operator and is called with the same syntax. So if we write:

```
function ">" (p1, p2 : person) return boolean is
begin
  return (p1. age > p2. age) ; —— this ">"
  —— is the operator "greater than" defined for values
```

```
      —— of the type of "p1.age" and
      —— does not denote a recursive call of the function.
   end ;
```

then the call

   older (johnson, harris) ;

may now be written as

   johnson > harris

The resulting infix notation is convenient in a number of cases, e.g. in the case of *** for matrix multiplication.

Overloading is not only possible for operators but also for enumeration literals (see 5.2.13) and identifiers used as function- or procedure names. However the ambiguity introduced in this manner may be impossible to resolve. In such cases, it is necessary to provide additional information which enables the compiler to correctly translate the program. For example (see 5.2.13):

   day'(sun)

makes *sun* unambiguously the enumeration literal of type *day*. Even with this additional qualification overloading may not be resolvable, for example for subprograms with the same names and parameter types. If this is the case, the program is illegal.

Actual parameters may be given in two ways: either *positional* (the conventional FORTRAN or Pascal style) or *named* as used in many job control languages. The named notation uses the name of the formal parameter and the $=>$ symbol for the association of the parameter with the actual value:

   older (p2 $=>$ harris , p1 $=>$ johnson) ;

Named parameter association can be combined with the facility to provide default values for **in** parameters, allowing the omission of actual parameter values in the call. The subprogram heading must contain initial values for such parameters which are then used in a call of that subprogram when no corresponding actual parameters are provided.

Given the enumeration types

> type *kind* is *(cream, black)* ;
> type *sweetener* is *(sugar, saccharine, none)* ;

and the procedure heading

> **procedure** *coffee (how : kind := cream, with : sweetener := sugar)* ;

then the the following three calls:

> *coffee (black, with => none)* ;
> *coffee (how => black)* ;
> *coffee* ;

are equivalent with the following three calls respectively:

> *coffee (black, none)* ;
> *coffee (black, sugar)* ;
> *coffee (cream, sugar)* ;

5.5   PACKAGES AND PRIVATE TYPES

5.5.1   Introduction

The package in Ada serves similar purposes to the module of Modula and CHILL, viz. the hiding (or rather, the protection) of internal types, variables, constants and subprograms and the definition of abstract data types. The two purposes mentioned above are dealt with in the following two subsections. First the hiding of information is described and then the mechanism for the definition of abstract data types is discussed.

5.5.2   Information hiding

A package appears in two parts, a specification part and an implementation part. The types, variables, constants and subprograms named in the specification part are exported for use in other packages; the names that only appear in the implementation part of the package are strictly local to the package.

A schematic example, comparable with the schematic example for a module in Modula (section 3.5) is as follows:

```
package name is — — package specification
    type t1 is ... ; — — exported type
    c : constant t1 ; — — exported constant of type t1
    v1 : t1 ; — — exported variable
    procedure p1 (...) ; — — exported procedure
    procedure p2 (...) ; — — exported procedure
end name ;
```

```
package body name is — — package implementation
    type t2 is ... ; — — type local to package
    v2 : t2 ; — — local variable
    v3 : t1 ; — — local variable
    procedure p1 (....) is begin . . end p1 ; — — implementation of p1
    procedure p2 (....) is begin . . end p2 ; — — implementation of p2
    procedure p3 (....) is begin . . end p3 ; — — local procedure
begin
    — — statements for initialization
end name ;
```

The separation of the specification from the implementation (body) of a package provides the means to supply all the necessary information for the use of the facilities defined in the package, without disclosing the implementation details.

In order for a package to make use of entities declared in another package, that package must explicitly be referenced in a **with** clause. The use of such a clause makes all the names defined in the package specification accessible. For example:

```
with name ; — — import all the exported names from package "name"
package import is
    — — declaration of names exported to other packages
    v : name.t1 ; — — variable declaration of type exported from "name"
end import ;
```

Note that in the variable declaration of *v* the name of the package exporting the type *t1* must be given as a qualifier. Names in referenced packages (i.e. through qualifiers) can be made directly visible, i.e. without qualification by utilizing the **use** clause. For example:

```
with name ;
use name ;
package import is
   v : t1 ; — — no qualification needed now
end import ;
```

The package as outlined above hides information about the implementation of exported names and can be used to implement abstract data types. However it does not limit the operations on values of exported types to those defined in the package itself. If more protection is required, the *private type* must be used.

Note that this extra protection is given in Modula by enforcing additional rules for exported types (see section 3.5). In CHILL this is achieved to some extent via the *newmode* concept and the *forbid* clause (see sections 4.2.13 and 4.5).

5.5.3   Private types

For values of a private type the only allowable operations are those exported explicitly from the package specification (except for comparison and assignment, see below). The specification part of a package is split in two sections: a *visible* part and a *private* part. Types that are part of an abstract data type must be named in the visible part and defined in the private part. An example of such a definition could be:

```
package abstract is
   type t1 is ... ; — — as before, a normal type
   type tpr is private ; — — exported type but hidden definition
   type tlp is limited private ; — — as above
   cpr : constant tpr ; — — exported constant
private
   type tpr is ... ; — — definition of private type
   type tlp is ... ; — — definition of limited private type
```

```
  cpr : constant tpr := ... ; — — give value of constant
end abstract ;
```

With the exception of the comparison for (in)equality and assignment
no operations are implicitly defined for private types. When there is
a need for other operations, such as, for example, addition, then a
function for that operation must be declared in the visible part of the
package specification. For example:

```
package abstract is
  type tpr is private ;
  function "+" (arg1, arg2 : tpr) return tpr ;
  — — specifies that addition for variables of the private
  — — type "tpr" can be used outside the package
   . . .
private
   . . .
end abstract ;
```

The body of the function + must be given in the package body.

Limited private types offer even stronger protection, as for such types
the (in)equality operation is not available either. A limited private type
is, as far as the allowed operations are concerned, comparable with a
type exported from a module in Modula.

Constants of a private type must be named in the visible part of
the package specification, but cannot be given their value there as
this would contradict the private nature of the type. Therefore, the
association between the name and the value is deferred to the private
part of the specification (see also 5.2.3).

The example key_manager as programmed in Modula and CHILL (see
3.5 and 4.5) is now programmed in Ada. Because the assignment and
equality operator have to be available outside the package, a key will
be defined as a private type, and not as a limited private type. Hence
the assignment and the equality operations do not have to be defined in
the package (as is necessary in Modula). Apart from the type key (with
an unknown structure outside the package), the variable available and
the procedure get_key are available for users of the package.

```
package key_ manager is
  type key is private ;
  available : boolean ;
  procedure get_ key ( k : out key) ;
private
  type key is new integer range 0..99 ;
end key_ manager ;

package body key_ manager is
  present_ key : key := key'first ;
  available := present_ key < key'last ;
  procedure get_ key ( k : out key) is
  begin
    if not available
      then k := key'first ;
      else
        present_ key := key'succ (present_ key) ;
        k := present_ key ;
        available := present_ key < key'last ;
    end if ;
  end get_ key ;
end key_ manager ;
```

Outside the package, the names mentioned in the visible part can be used through qualification with the name of the package, for example (compare with 3.5):

```
front_ door, back_ door : key_ manager.key ;
if key_ manager.available
  then key_ manager.get_ key (front_ door) ;
end if ;
if back_ door /= front_ door
  then back_ door := front_ door ;
end if ;
```

The assignment

```
front_ door := 6 ;
```

which is legal in CHILL, but illegal in Modula, is also illegal in Ada.

5.6 TASKS

A task is a sequential program part that may be executed concurrently with other tasks. This concurrent execution may be done by different processors or by interleaved execution on a single processor. This is similar to the process concept in both Modula and CHILL.

A task has to be declared; syntactically a task declaration looks like a package declaration. It consists of two parts:

- the task specification contains all information needed to use the task, viz. the names and parameters of the *entries* of the task (see section 5.7).

- the task body contains the statements that are executed upon activation of the task.

If the specification of a task is given in the declarative part of a package, then the body of that task must be specified in the declarative part of the corresponding package body.

Unlike packages, tasks are considered to be of a (task) type, for example:

```
task type sync is —— task type specification
   entry together; —— visible to the outer world
end sync ;
task body sync is —— task body, defining the operations
   —— statements
end sync ;
```

This allows the creation of a number of tasks (more precisely: task objects) of type *sync*. One such an object is declared by

```
s : sync ;
```

When only one task of a given task type is needed, the task type declaration and the task object declaration may be combined by omitting the keyword **type** in the task type declaration. For objects of a task type, assignment and comparison are not available, comparable with the situation for limited private types.

Both activation and termination of a task are done implicitly. A task automatically becomes active when the directly enclosing unit (which may be a task itself) reaches the **begin** that follows the declarations of that unit. Normal termination of a task occurs when either its execution reaches the end of its task body or a **terminate** alternative is selected in a **select** statement (see section 5.7). A block, subprogram or task can only be left when all tasks that were spawned as a consequence of the execution of that block, subprogram or task have terminated their execution.

This implicit activation and termination is used in the example program for the robot, introduced in section 3.6. The robot-arm has a separate motor for each of the three dimensions and the movements of the three motors are controlled concurrently. A position is completely characterized by three coordinates:

```
type position is
  record
    x, y, z : integer ;
  end record ;
```

and there is a number of positions, stored in an array:

```
max : constant := 30 ;
positions : array (1..max) of position ;
```

All those positions are "touched upon" sequentially by a simple loop:

```
for i in positions'range
  loop
    move_ arm (positions (i)) ;
  end loop ;
```

The concurrent part is implemented in three tasks within the procedure *move_ arm*:

```
procedure move_ arm (new_ position : in position) is
  task move_ x ;
  task move_ y ;
  task move_ z ;

  task body move_ x is
    . . .
```

```
begin
   —— statements controlling the x— motor
end move_x ;

task body move_y is
   . . .
begin
   —— statements controlling the y— motor
end move_y ;

task body move_z is
   . . .
begin
   —— statements controlling the z— motor
end move_z ;

begin —— move_x, move_y and move_z are activated
   —— implicitly in some order
   null ; —— the non— empty notation for the empty statement
end move_arm ;
   —— await termination of move_x, move_y and move_z
```

5.7   COMMUNICATION BETWEEN TASKS

Communication between tasks in Ada is done by a mechanism in which a kind of procedure defined in one task can be called from another task. The working of this type of communication is explained using the following schematic program part with two tasks, $t1$ and $t2$:

```
task t1 is
   entry meet_me (p : parameter_type) ;
end t1 ;

task body t1 is
   . . .
   accept meet_me (p : parameter_type) do
      —— body of accept statement
   end meet_me ;
end t1 ;
```

task *t2 ;* — — *no visible part*

task body *t2* **is**

  . . .

    t1. meet__ me (actual parameter) ; — — *entry call*
  end *t2 ;*

Task *t2* calls the **entry** *meet__ me* in task *t1*. The body of *meet__ me*
is specified in the **accept** statement in the body of *t1*. The **entry**
declaration has to be given in the visible part of *t1* and is similar
to a procedure heading. It includes the specification of the formal
parameters. Task *t2* establishes the communication by calling:

    t1. meet__ me (actual parameter) ;

However the body of the **accept** statement *meet__ me* can only be executed when the flow of control in *t1* has reached the **accept** statement. For this reason the communication mechanism in Ada is also
called: *rendezvous*. Whichever task reaches its communication statement (**entry** call or **accept**) first waits for the other. At the moment of
the rendezvous formal and actual parameters (if any) are associated as
in procedure calls. The calling task is held up while the body of the
accept statement is executed and is only allowed to continue when the
accept statement is completed. The two tasks then continue on their
separate ways.

From the caller's point of view there is no difference between a procedure
call and an **entry** call. In this respect, the body of an **accept** statement
can be compared with the body of a procedure. Note that the rendezvous mechanism is asymmetric: within the calling task the identity of
the task containing the **entry** is known, but not vice versa.

For a given **entry** declaration there may be more than one **accept** statement, each with its own body. In this respect there is a fundamental
difference with a procedure, which may only have one body belonging
to a procedure heading.

An address may be specified for an **entry**, in which case the **entry** is
linked to a hardware interrupt. For example, assume that the task
move__ x (see section 5.6) actually controls the x-direction motor through
a memory mapped input/output address. Assume also that when the
motor has actually reached its position, an interrupt is generated. This

interrupt can be associated with an **accept** statement. The task *move_ x* can now be programmed as follows:

```
task move_ x is
  entry x_ interrupt ;
  for x_ interrupt use at 16# 20000# ;
end move_ x ;

task body move_ x is
  x_ motor : address ; — — assume address suitably defined
  for x_ motor use at 16# 4000# ;
begin
  x_ motor := new_ position.x ; — — output position
  accept x_ interrupt ; — — wait for interrupt
end move_ x ;
```

Associated with each **entry** there is a -possibly empty- queue of waiting **entry** calls which are processed on a first come, first served basis. Note that a task can only be on one queue since it can only call one **entry** at a time.

A **select** statement allows conditional selection of branches in which **accept** statements can be placed. Every branch may be preceded by a condition, called a guard. The execution of a **select** statement results in the execution of exactly one of the branches. The selection of a branch is governed by the following rules:

- When the **select** statement is entered, all guards are evaluated.

- Only those branches are considered whose guard is true. Such branches are said to be open. There must be at least one open branch.

- Of the open branches one is selected at random for which a rendezvous is possible, i.e. for which a calling task is waiting.

- If no rendezvous is possible, execution of the task is suspended until an **entry** with an **accept** statement in an open branch is called. Note that the guards are not evaluated again.

The classical bounded buffer as programmed in section 3.7 is used to illustrate the **select** statement. The program has to ensure that reading from (i.e. *get*) and writing into (*put*) the buffer are mutually exclusive and that the buffer cannot be over-filled or under-emptied.

```
package exchange is
  task buffer_ task is
    entry get (c : out char) ;
    entry put (c : in char) ;
  end buffer_ task ;
end exchange ; —— end of package specification

package body exchange is
  task body buffer_ task is
    max : constant := 10 ;
    container : array (1..max) of char ;
    in, out : integer := 1 ;
    n : integer := 0 ;
  begin
    loop
      select
        when n < max =>
          —— guard to ensure that the buffer is not over—filled
          accept put (c : in char) do
            container (in) := c ;
          end put ;
          in := in mod max + 1 ; n := n + 1 ;
      or
        when n > 0 =>
          —— guard to ensure that the buffer is not under— emptied
          accept get (c : out char) do
            c := container (out) ;
          end get ;
          out := out mod max + 1 ; n := n − 1 ;
      end select ;
    end loop ;
  end buffer_ task ;
end exchange ;
```

In the case that both guards are true, various possibilities arise. If neither *get* nor *put* has been called, then the task waits until one is called; if one of the two has been called then the appropriate branch is taken; if both have been called then one branch is selected in an unspecified but fair manner.

The example previously given in Modula (see section 3.7), i.e. a schema of a complete program, including the task declarations for *producer* and *consumer*, reads in Ada:

```
with exchange ;
use exchange ;

package give_ and_ take is
    —— this is a main program schema
    —— hence visible part is empty
end give_ and_ take ;

package body give_ and_ take is
    task type producer ; —— two instances required
    task consumer ; —— only one instance required

    task body producer is
      ch : char ;
    begin
      loop
        . . put(ch) ; . . —— entry call on buffer_ task
      end loop ;
    end producer ;

    task body consumer is
      ch : char ;
    begin
      loop
        . . get(ch) ; . . —— entry call on buffer_ task
      end loop ;
    end consumer ;

    p1, p2 : producer ; —— two instances of producer required

begin
    —— producers, consumer and buffer_ task
    —— are activated in some order
end give_ and_ take ;
```

accept statements may also be used merely to synchronize tasks, if no

data have to be transferred. In that case there are no parameters and
the body of the **accept** statement is omitted. The **entry** declaration and
accept statement degenerate into

> **entry** *beep ;*
> **accept** *beep ;*

and the call is simply

> *beep ;*

Evidently, when there are more task objects of the same task type,
calls have to specify to which task they are referring. This is done by
qualifying the name of the entry with the name of the task (object),
e.g.

> *t1.beep ;*

Ada allows more possibilities in the **accept** and **select** statements than
those outlined above. A limit may be placed on the length of time a
task is allowed to wait for a rendezvous to occur. In a **select** statement,
terminate may be used as an alternative. This enables the task to
terminate if no rendezvous is possible and suitable conditions hold.

5.8 EXCEPTIONS

Like CHILL, Ada provides a means for dealing with errors or other
exceptional situations. At the end of a program unit but belonging
to that unit, a number of exception handlers may be specified. These
handlers are responsible for handling the exceptions that are raised
within the program unit. If such an error is raised during the execution
of a statement of that program unit, control is immediately transferred
to the corresponding handler. After the execution of the emergency
action specified within the exception handler, the program unit is left,
in other words: control is not returned to the point where the exception
was raised. An exception has to be declared in an **exception** declaration.

Exception handling is a dynamic mechanism. If a handler is not provided for a particular exception in a given program unit then that
unit is left and the exception is re-raised prior to the execution of the
first statement dynamically following the program unit. This process

is known as exception propagation. For a procedure as a program unit, this implies that the exception is propagated to its caller. It is possible to provide an **others** exception handler to catch all exceptions that are not handled otherwise.

For embedded computer applications it is essential that all error conditions (i.e. violations of the language rules) which cannot be checked at compile time, raise an exception at run time. Therefore there is a number of predefined exceptions, such as constraint_error, numeric_error. A user may declare additional exceptions. An exception can be raised explicitly by a **raise** statement; for the user defined exceptions, this is the only way to raise them.

To illustrate the application of user-defined exceptions, the example *traffic_handling* from section 4.8 is programmed in Ada. The procedure may raise one of three exceptions; one of them (*abort*) is handled within the procedure, the other two (*congestion* and *time_out*) are propagated to the dynamically enclosing program unit:

```
—— assume "congestion" and "time_out"
—— have been declared as exceptions
procedure traffic_handling is
  abort : exception ;
begin
  if —— some condition
    then raise abort ;
  end if ;
  if —— some other condition
    then raise congestion ;
    else raise time_out ;
  end if ;
exception
  when abort => —— some action ;
end traffic_handling ;
```

A notable difference with CHILL is the fact that the non-local exceptions are not mentioned explicitly as a kind of parameter in the heading of the procedure. The property that an exception is non-local follows implicity from the fact that it is not declared locally.

If it is required to handle the non-local exceptions in the immediate environment of the call statement, a block is created for this purpose:

```
begin
  traffic_ handling ;
exception
  when congestion => —— some statements ;
  when time_ out => —— some other statements ;
end ;
```

The precise rules for associating the appropriate exception handler with
a raised exception are rather complicated (depending, amongst other
things, on whether the exception was raised during the elaboration of
a declaration or not); furthermore, the interaction between exceptions
and tasking (not discussed here) is complex.

5.9   SEPARATE COMPILATION

The text of a program can be submitted to the compiler in one or more
parts. The part of a program that can be compiled separately from
other parts is called a compilation unit. Compilation units fall into
two categories: *library units* and *subunits*.

A *library unit* can be either the specification or the body of a subprogram or the specification of a package. After compilation, the compiled code is put in the program library. Compilation units can use the
already compiled units in the program library by mentioning their name
in a **with** clause (note the difference with Pascal's **with** statement). For
example:

```
with complex_ numbers ;
  —— imports all names of visible part of "complex_ numbers"
use complex_ numbers ;
  —— makes these names visible without qualification
procedure solve (a, b, c : real; z1, z2 : out complex) is
begin
  ....
end solve ;
```

The package specification of *complex_ numbers* must be in the program
library when the above unit is submitted for compilation. A program
library contains all information about exported types, subprograms,
etc. Hence the compiler can check whether the use of imported names

in a unit submitted for compilation complies with their definitions in the program library. If a library unit is changed, recompilation is necessary for that unit, and generally for all units that mention this unit in a **with** clause.

Compilation units can also be *subunits*. This provides the possibility to defer the compilation of bodies of packages, subprograms and tasks which are embedded in a compilation unit. The specifications of packages, tasks and subprograms must be given in the compilation unit, but the bodies can be marked with: **is separate**. This allows program development by hierarchical decomposition, for example:

```
package body stack is
    max : constant := 100 ;
    s : array (1..max) of real ;
    ptr : integer range 0..max := 0 ;
    procedure push (x : real) is separate ;
    function pop return real is separate ;
    end stack ;
```

The keywords **is separate** indicate that both *push* and *pop* will be compiled separately as subunits. The visibilty of names in the separately compiled subunits is exactly as if these units had not been separated from the "parent" compilation unit. Compilation of a subunit can take place after the compilation of the unit to which it belongs. The name of this unit must appear before the text of the subunit, for example:

```
separate (stack) ;
procedure push (x : real) is
begin
    ...
end push ;
```

5.10   GENERICS

The type system of Ada imposes strong requirements on the types of objects that can be used in expressions and assignment statements. This "strong typing" makes it impossible to write a general procedure performing some operation on values or variables regardless of their types, e.g. to swap the values of two variables. The "general" must

thus be understood in the sense that such a procedure would per-
form the swap, regardless of the type of the actual variables, provided
they are the same. Nevertheless in order to allow the writing of such
general procedures, Ada allows some kind of parametrization in *generic
program units*.

A *generic program unit* is a template for an ordinary program unit.
The template itself cannot be executed because certain information is
lacking. An ordinary program unit can be made by instantiation (i.e.
making an instance) of the generic progam unit. For instantiation of a
generic program unit its parameters must be supplied. The declaration
of a generic program unit -either a subprogram or a package- is very
similar to a normal program unit declaration. An example of a generic
subprogram declaration is:

```
generic
   type elem is private ;
procedure exchange (u, v : in out elem) is
   t : elem ; — — the generic formal type
begin
   t := u ;
   u := v ;
   v := t ;
end exchange ;
```

The type declaration *elem* is a generic parameter.

A generic actual parameter must be supplied for each generic formal
parameter when the generic package or subprogram is instantiated. As
for subprograms, parameters can be given either in positional or in
named form. An example of the creation of two instances of the generic
subprogram *swap* is as follows:

```
procedure swap is new exchange (elem => integer) ;
procedure swap is new exchange (character) ;
   — — note that swap is now overloaded
```

Now *swap* can be used as follows:

```
c1, c2 : character ;
i1, i2 : integer ;
```

swap (c1, c2) ; — — swaps characters
swap (i1, i2) ; — — swaps integers

and thus the desired generality has been achieved through an extra
level of abstraction.

As generic parameters also subprograms may be specified:

generic
    type *item* **is private** *; — — generic type parameter*
    with function *"*" (u, v : item)* **return** *item ;*
      — — generic subprogram parameter
    package *mult* **is** ...

When instantiating, the actual parameters have to be supplied for the
generic type *item* and for the generic function ***. For example, assuming
matrix_ mpy has been defined as:

function *matrix_ mpy (m1, m2 : matrix)* **return** *matrix ;*

an instantiation of the package *mult* could be:

package *multiply* **is new** *mult (matrix, "*"* => *matrix_ mpy) ;*

It is possible to specify default values for generic parameters. In the
example given above this could e.g. be accomplished as follows:

generic
    type *item* **is private** *;*
    with function *"*" (u, v : item)* **return** *item* **is** <> *;*
    package ...

The box symbol <> indicates that if the actual parameter for the
generic subprogram is omitted when instantiating the package, a subprogram with a matching specification is used. There must be exactly
one such subprogram visible at the point of instantiation.

BIBLIOGRAPHY

This bibliography is restricted to the most important references. It contains the definitions of the four languages and one or two good textbooks per language (if available).

There are numerous textbooks on Pascal, but most of them are based on the original Pascal definition written by Wirth. The chosen textbook is based on ISO Pascal. The original User Manual and Report by Wirth has also been included in the list.

Textbooks on Modula are not available, but there is one on Modula-2.

For CHILL there exists an introduction to CHILL, published by the CCITT (Comite Consultatif International Telegraphique et Telephonique). It does not cover the full language. An official User Manual is also published by the CCITT.

Textbooks on Ada are starting to appear. Some care should be taken because the language definition was changed as a result of the ANSI standardization process. At present no books are based on the ANSI standard.

1. Specification for computer programming language Pascal.
    British Standards Institute, BS 6192 (1982)

2. J. Welsh, J. Elder
    Introduction to Pascal (2nd edition).
    Prentice-Hall (1982)

3. K. Jensen, N. Wirth
    Pascal User Manual and Report.
    Springer Verlag (1974)

4. N. Wirth
    Modula, a language for modular programming.
    Software, Practice and Experience, Vol 7, 3-35 (1977)

5. N. Wirth
    Modula-2
    Springer Verlag (1983)

6. CCITT High Level Language (CHILL), Recommendation Z.200
    CCITT, Geneva (1980)

7. Introduction to CHILL
    CCITT, Geneva (1980)

8. CHILL User Manual
    CCITT, Geneva (1983)

9. Reference Manual for the Ada Programming Language.
    U.S. Dept. of Defense, Mil-Std 1815a (1983)

10. J.G.P. Barnes
    Programming in Ada
    Addison-Wesley (1982)

INDEX

abstract data type 8,46,47,88,114,124,126
abstraction 7
accept statement 132
access type 113
activation of a task 129
Ada 9,12,38,104
Ada programming environment 11,105
aggregate 108,112
ALGOL 60 8,10,29
ALGOL 68 104
allocator 114
ANSI 36,105
APSE 105
array 21,42,71,108
array aggregate 108
array attribute 109
array dimensions 21,71,108
array slice 72,109
array tuple 72
array type 20,21,42,71,108,115
assembly language 10,39
assert statement 36,85
at 116
awaited signal 54

base type 116
begin end block 85
bit string 24
bit string type 72
bits type 41
bitset type 62
block 85
block statement 118
Blue 104
bool 70
boolean type 16,41,70,107
bound reference 76

Bourgonjon 12
box symbol 122,141
branch in select statement 133
Brinch Hansen 37
buffer 91,93,95
busy waiting 54

call statement 29,87
cardinal type 62
case statement 28,36,43,82,118
cause statement 100
CCITT 12,38,66
char 16,70
character string type 72
character type 16,41,70,107
CHILL 9,12,38,66
CHILL programming environment 11,67
CII-Honeywell Bull 12,105
COBOL 10
compiler 11
compound statement 28,42
computer aided manufacturing 10
concatenation 73,110,118
concealed name 89
concurrency 9,35,37,39,49,129
Concurrent Pascal 37
configuration management 11
conformant array parameter 34,36,44
const 18,69
constant attribute 106
constant definition 18,68,106
constraint error exception 137
continue statement 94
coroutine 63

data structuring 8,10
data type 8
dcl 69
deadlock 54
debugger 11
decision table 82,119

declare 118
default value for discriminant 113
default value for generic parameter 141
default value for subprogram parameter 123
deferred constant 107,127
define 45
defining occurrence 89,103
definition module 64
delay statement 94
delta 108
Department of Defense 12,104
dereferencing 26,69,77,114
derived type 116
design 11
device communication 57
device module 39,41,58,63
device process 41,58
digits 108
directive 115
discrete type 16
discriminant 110
dispose 27,114
distributed system 40,93,97
do statement 83
DoD 12
doio statement 58
double precision 35
driver 60,64,98
duration type 107
dynamic memory allocation 26,76,114
dynamic string 35
dynamic type 71,77

editor 11
elsif part 43,82,118
embedded computer system 10,12,35,37,66,104,137
empty exception 100
entry declaration 129,132
enumeration type 16,18,42,69,107,114
event 94
exception 40,85,99,136

exception formal 102
exception handler 100,136
exception propagation 101,137
exit statement 36,43,83,120
exponentiation 35,118
export 63
expression 117
external file 36

file type 20,25,42,71,108
first attribute 109
fixed point type 108
flexible array bounds 33
floating point type 107,108
for clause 83,119
for statement 28,42,43
forbid clause 88,90,126
formal exceptions 102
FORTRAN 8,10,15,19,20,24,26,27,28,34
free reference 76
function 29,44,85,87,121

generic parameter 140
generic program unit 140
generics 9,139
global variables 32,48
goto statement 28,43,84,120
grant 87
grant forbid 90
grant pervasive 90
Green 104
guard 133

high 44
Hoare 38

Ichbiah 12,105
if statement 28,42,43,82,118
imaginary outermost process 91,92
implementation module 64
import 63

in out parameter 86,121
in parameter 86,121
independent compilation 8,103
index 21,71,108
information hiding 8,47,124
initialization of variables 35,45,47,70,106
input 10,25,35,39,58,63,108,115,132
instance 50,91,97
int 70
integer type 16,41,70,107
interface module 39,41,51,63,94
interface procedure 51
interrupt 35,37,39,58,132
interrupt priority 58
intersection 23,76
Ironman 104
ISO Pascal 11,15,30,33,35,36,44,81

last attribute 109
length attribute 109
library 90,103
library unit 138
life-time of software product 11
limited private type 117,127
linked list 27
local variables 32
location 69
loop statement 43,119
low 44
low level facilities 63

mailbox 95
main module 64
maintenance 11
Modula 12,37,39,105
Modula-2 12,37,40,62
modular design 7
module 39,41,45,63,87,102,124
mutual exclusion 52,53,55,93,94

natural type 107

new 26,114
newmode 80,126
null statement 119
numeric applications 10
numeric error exception 137

open branch in select 133
operating system kernel 12,40
operating systems 35,37
orthogonality 7
others in case statement 119
others in exception handling 137
others in variant record 111
otherwise clause 36
out parameter 86,121
output 10,25,35,39,58,63,108,115,132
overflow exception 100
overloading 117
overloading of identifiers 123
overloading of operators 122

pack 20,79,106,115
package 124
package private part 126
package visible part 126
parameter attributes 86,121
parameter passing by reference 31,85
parameter passing by value 30,31,85,86,121
parameter passing by variable 30,86
parameters actual 30,44,86,121
parameters default values 123
parameters formal 30,44,85,121
parameters named association 123,140
parameters positional association 123,140
parent type 116
Pascal 7,11,14,104,105
Pascal extensions 15,34
Pascal-plus 38
Philips 12
piecewise compilation 102
PL/1 104

pointer type 16,26,42,69,76,105,113
portability 18,41
Portal 38
pos 80
powerset mode 69
powerset type 76
pragma directive 115
pred 19
predefined type 16,41,70,107
pretty printer 11
priority of process 58
private part 107,126
private type 107,114,126
proc 78,85
procedure 29,44,85,121
procedure as parameter 78
procedure type 62,78
process 37,39,41,49,91,129
process communication 51,93,131
process control 12
process creation 64
process declaration 51,91
process instance 50,91,97
process parameters 92
process start 50,92
process statement 50
process terminate 92
producer and consumer 52,95,134,135
program 34,51,93
program data base 11
program design 11
program library 138
program maintenance 11
program testing 11
programming support environment 10,11,67,105

qualification 62,103,126
qualified 62
qualified expression 117

raise statement 137

random access file 26,35,36
range 107
range attribute 119
range constraint 107
range type 70
rangefail exception 100
read 70,106
read file 25
read only 48,70
readability 7
real type 16,41,71,107
real-time FORTRAN 10
real-time systems 9,10,12,37,39
receive buffer 95
receive signal (CHILL) 97
record aggregate 112
record discriminant 110
record field 22,74,90,110
record tuple 75
record type 20,21,42,69,73,108,110,115
record variant 22,74,110
recursive procedure 34
Red 104
ref 69,77
reference mode 69
region 91,93,94
regular process 58
rendezvous 132
repeat until statement 28,43
representation specification 79,106,114
requirements specification 11
reset file 25
return 78
returns 78
rewrite file 25
row 77,86
RTL/2 19,20,23,24,26,27,28,29,34

scope 32,44,47
seize 87
select statement 133

semaphore 37
send buffer 95
send signal (CHILL) 97
send signal (Modula) 51,54
separate compilation 8,11,36,39,64,102,138
set mode (CHILL) 69
set type (CHILL) 70,76
set type (Pascal) 20,23,41,42,69,108,118
shared variable 39,51,93
short circuit control form 117
signal (CHILL) 91,93,97
signal (Modula) 41,51,54,94
simple type 16,41,70,105,107
slice 72,73,109
start statement 92
statement closing symbol 43,82,118
statements 28,42,82,117
static type 71
Steelman 104
stepwise refinement 65
Stoneman 105
string 21,35,69,107
string slice 73
string type 71,72,108,109
struct 69,74
structure mode 69,73
structured constant 35,69,107
structured type 16,20,42,71,105,108
subarray 72
subprogram 29,44,85,121
subrange 70,107
subrange type 16,20,42
subscript 21
subsetting of language 13
substring 73
subtype 107,116
succ 19
syn 69
synchronization 51,93
synmode 69,70
synonym 69

system module 63
systems programming 10,40

tag field 22,75,111
tagfail exception 100
task 129
task activation 129
task communication 131
task entry 129
task termination 130
task type 117,129
telecommunication systems 12
terminate alternative in select 136
testing 11
text file 25
text reference 103
top-down design 65
transfer 63
type 8
type compatibility 80,106,116
type conversion 81,116
type definition 16,41,68,107
type derived 106,116
type discrete 16
type parent 116
type predefined 16,41,70,107
type simple 16,41,70,107
type user defined 16,70,107

UCSD Pascal 14
unconstrained array type 109,122
union 23,76
upper 72,73
use 45,115

value parameters 30
var 17,69
variable declaration 16,70,106
variable initialization 35,45,47,70,106
variable parameters 30
variable shared 39,51,93

variant record 22,74,110
version control 11
visibility 45,88,126
visible part 126

wait signal (Modula) 51,54,94
weakly visible 90
when clause 43
while clause 83,84,119
while statement 28,42,43
Wirth 11,12,14,33,36,39,40
with clause 83,84,121,138
with statement 29,42,44
write file 25
writeability 7

Yellow 104